The Haunting of Sierra Sky -

The Secret Life of a Spirit Rescuer

Tina Louise Niemi

ISBN: 1505993504
ISBN-13: 978-1505993509

Dolphinhugs4u2
Stringer, MS 39481

Dedication

I would like to dedicate this book to everyone that has ever lost a loved one. I would also include anyone that has ever been touched by the Spirit realm. You are not crazy and life does go on.

Sierra Sky

Table of Contents

ACKNOWLEDGMENTS

This book would not be possible if it wasn't for the support of my family and friends.

Ama Nazra my mentor, she took me under her wings and guided me on my path, she taught me about demonology our Arch Angel Michael and negative energy! She is the reason I am a Spirit Rescuer.

Tracy Rector, together we walked this path you have taught me to be strong face my demons but have respect for the spirit realm.

Enixer, my soul sister, with her extreme empathy my angel eyes a visionary she has shown me many obstacles that come my way she sees and warns I trust her insight.

Marlys, with her ability of clairvoyance, and who guides us through our photos to the spirits who need healing. With her amazing insight Marlys creates the picture she is also a fierce protector and friend. A key member of my team.

Cyndie Lepori, My wing man when it comes to clearing negative energy, and sending spirits home, for without her this journey would not be possible.

Phoenix Rising, a protector in the other realms of spirit. He has been here from almost the beginning.

Valerie, the Paranormal Research Society taught me so much about my gifts and got me though some hard life's lessons. I thank you for your loving friendship and support these past five years.

To my Daughters and Grandson each of you has special gifts. I look forward to the day when you realize them and assist with the Teams efforts as some of you are now. I love you all dearly.

Golden Phoenix, and Lance Oliver, they are my teachers and guides in the practice of Reiki healing. They both have attuned me to different systems of Reiki.

But most of all, I want to thank my family. Especially my mother and father, without their guidance I would have been lost, possibly forever. They were there for me even in the darkest of times. My parent's strength and natural gifts and protective nature enabled me to move forward.

Finally, I would like to thank all of the families who contributed their stories in the pages of this book. To my guides to are always there reminding me of my path. This journey has been one of tremendous growth and sacrifice. A journey I wouldn't have changed, my understanding lies solely in the spirits that have come into my life to show how Spirit Rescue truly is important.

Preface

The accounts in this book are from actual
events. Some of the names have been changed either
due to lack of permission or to protect the
innocent. My hope is you find these amazing and show
you how I got to become a Spirit Rescuer.

Five years ago I would have told you were crazy if you
had said I would be where I am right now. Writing this
book validates to me that I do not need of counseling.

For years I really thought, "What did I do to deserve
this?" After a realization, a rebirth I now know my
path. I know I am not crazy. The pushing, the poking,
the voices are in fact are important lessons for
me. Here I am stronger and more aware of the multi
dimensions of this existence just a short five years
later.

I have accepted the Divine's will and I take this journey
with pride. I feel honored to be asked to do so. I also
feel honored that you the reader would take to time
and share my journey. I hope for those beginning their
journey as a Spirit Rescuer that this will let you know
that you are not crazy

This is my journey thus far, I am

Sierra Sky

Chapter One
A Haunting in Fort Worth

April 2004

My former husband and I, were going to Cisco, Texas to visit his parents. His family had a farm along with orchards. We were going to help them pick tomatoes to be packaged, and then take the harvest to Abilene, Texas to sell at the Farmers Market. On our trip to sell the vegetables, we passed through the town of Thurber, Tx. Thurber had originally been a coal mining town when business was booming during the 1800's. Today it is a ghost town. While passing through, we noticed a historical marker and decided to pull off of the freeway. A strong feeling came over me, and I knew I had to find the town cemetery. After 30 minutes of looking desperately, I found nothing, but I was not ready to give up the search that easily. The town of Thurber is known for the Smokestack Restaurant, and it is one of the original landmarks for Thurber. We pulled into the Smokestack parking lot, and we noticed that the road curved around the restaurant, so we followed it. There it was - silently waiting and inviting me, The Thurber Cemetery.

To enter the cemetery, we had to pull off the road, park the truck and then go under the fence. We followed a winding dirt road up a hill. At the top of the hill there was the cemetery. We had to cross a cattle guard to enter, but the gate was open- inviting us in. The first thing I saw floored me. There stood a wall with the names of children that had passed away during the diphtheria, and whooping cough epidemics that hit Texas in the 1800's through the early 1920's. As we walked around, I felt pulls on my heart strings and I knew that I had something I would need to do. There were hundreds of white crosses made of PVC pipe- unmarked graves, no names- just the cross showing that there were bodies buried here.

I was drawn to a grave. The headstone was not on the grave, but in the little fence that went around it. The headstone had been broken into pieces by vandals. The cruelty of the damage tore at my heart. I just stood there in shock. I felt so helpless! I did not know what I was supposed to do at this point, but I knew with certainty, that was that I was meant to be there. I knew the Lord knew my heart. I took a piece of the headstone that belonged to the little girl Maria; she was three years old when she passed from her childhood illness. I did not think about it, I only knew that I was to grab it. Little did I know what was in store for us. As we walked back down to the truck we tried to ponder so many questions. Why we were led here, what was our purpose?

The following day, I went to a friend's apartment and enjoy cooling off in the swimming pool. The Texas summer temperatures are frequently over 100, and a perfect way to cool down is by soaking in a pool.

There were three of us, sitting at the pool, watching our kids playing, and swimming. Mary is 26, a mother of two young boys, married but separated from her husband. My friend, Abigail, is a single, mother with three beautiful daughters. She is 32 years old. She is Wiccan and is following her path as a Solitary Practitioner. Mary was staying with Abigail till she got back on her feet. Mary also was learning the Wiccan ways and the process for being a sensitive.

I started to tell my friends of the trip to the cemetery and what had happened. My friend, Mary, was holding her son. We noticed, that he was looking over my shoulder- staring into the window of the apartment behind me. His attention would repeatedly be directed on something or someone in the window, each time we looked there was nothing there.

After telling them my story, I felt like a weight had been lifted off my chest. I was still troubled by my act of removing the headstone from the fence. I had not intended to take the headstone piece out of the cemetery. Was something making it so that I would have to come back?

For five days, I weighed the options in my mind. On the fifth day, I knew what I had to do- return to Thurber, that night- and make things right. Thurber is an hour drive from Fort Worth, so it would be after dark when I got there. Not a good idea considering I had only been there once. Something compelled me to go anyway. As I started walking down the winding road, I felt uneasy. This is Texas -no telling what wild animals would be lurking in the woods, not to mention ghosts. So I walked nervously, anxiously, with an urgency to make things right. It had been five days since I was able to return to the cemetery and I wanted to make sure the headstone made it back unmarked and safe in its final resting place. I had brought special items in my back pack that I wanted to leave as a peace offering with a sincere apology for any disturbance I had unthinkingly caused.

I placed the headstone back in its' original resting place. I then adorned the tiny fence with white roses, scattered red rose petals all over the grave and place an angel necklace in a white angel case for Maria. Leaving the cemetery that evening, I felt at peace with the knowledge that Maria and the others had forgiven me. As we drove back to Fort Worth, I could feel spirits around me. Something or someone was pulling on me, not sure how I knew, but I did.

Over the next couple of weeks, I had been feeling the children at the apartment. Money would go missing, things would be moved, and I would wake up every morning with my hair in a giant, tangled mess. To control my hair, I pulled it up into a ponytail. Even in this restricted style, people noticed that my hair was moving on its' own- as if being played with by unseen hands. While my own hands were at rest, the charms on my bracelet would jingle and clang.

 We decided to investigate who was "playing" with my hair and charms, along with the strange occurrences in the apartment. We had been without understanding for too long. We headed to the local Toys R Us, five minutes up the road. We were determined to get a

Ouija Board- that night. Nothing was going to get in the way of that happening. We would not stop searching, until we had found one. At the toy store, we bought a glow in the dark board. We had no clue as to what we were doing, but pulled the board out, as soon as we walked through the front door. I felt like the little boy, Alan, in the movie Jumanji. We did not know what would happen, but we felt like the spirits were calling out to us. We didn't know protection. We had no shields up, and we took no spiritual precautionary measures at all.

We pulled the game pieces out of the box. My ex went into the kitchen and returned with two whiskey shot glasses, a bottle of whiskey, and a candle. As we lit the candle, we each took a shot of whiskey for courage. We were so naive. Unknowingly, we had put ourselves in spiritual danger. I now know that if you're going to dabble with the unknown, absolutely no drugs or alcohol, and have a Bible close enough to grab. When one opens a portal, anything, good or evil can come through.

The first to come through was the little girl, Maria. While I was asking her questions, she told me that she had followed us home. We were the only ones that had been to the cemetery in a long time. As the session went on, we realized that there were many more children with her. The children wanted my ex and I to be their parents. We showed sensitivity and caring feelings. Even though, I did not know it at the time, I was receptive to spiritual beings. I think they knew who I was, however, I just wasn't aware what role my abilities would play out. We counted a total of eleven children in the house. My ex said that they were gathered around me as I was sitting on the couch. I remember I kept telling myself, that I wasn't afraid- for the energy had to be good, as they are just children. Since we had a physical connection to Thurber, we agreed to spiritually parent the spirit children.

As the days went on, I found myself spending more time alone with the board. I was talking on a regular basis to a masculine spirit who eventually disclosed his name as Ron. He was a firefighter, who had fallen off a ladder in Twin Tower number two. As the tower collapsed, he was crushed to his death. Although, I was surprised that he had wanted to communicate with me, it made sense. My entire living room had become a memorial of the Twin Towers, my tribute to the fallen and their families. My first piece of electric art was bought a week after 9/11, and the replica of the Twin Towers stood erected in my living room. On the far wall, I had twelve metal printing screens of the one year anniversary, from the local newspaper. The Fort Worth Star Telegram was on display in a line, by numerical sequence. The pages, a gift from a friend.

My curiosity was on high. I wanted to know more! I kept asking questions and found myself consumed and not wanting to do anything else but communicate through the board. The children came through for a while, then it was just Ron and I. In our nightly chats, Ron told me that my ex was doing drugs. I worked nights until two in the morning. He was always home alone. I wondered if he was getting high and then getting on the board. In his altered state, there was no control over who, or what, he was inviting into our apartment. There was a great deal of turmoil in our relationship, and we began to fight. I found out that he was stealing from me. That was the final straw, so I kicked him out. I was now alone and feeling vulnerable.

A few days later, while at work, I was walking through the bar when the chain I was wearing, fell off my neck. The necklace had been a gift, my in laws had brought back for me from the Holy Land, I didn't notice it was gone until hours later. When I discovered it was missing, a jolt went through me! At that moment, I knew I was unprotected. This necklace also had a lot of sentimental value for me. I had not had that necklace off my neck until that night. I had worn it continuously for 10 years. I had a lot of faith, but now that my "protection" necklace was gone, I started panicking. I looked all over the bar. Finally, I gave up and went back to the Managers office to report my missing necklace. I described it to her, and she said, holding up a gold chain, "this what you're looking for?" My heart swelled, it was found! I immediately put it back on. I now felt protected again.

I went back to work and a transformation began. I was giving spiritual readings for my friends. I was sharing information about their lives that they didn't know. I was receiving so many messages from multiple sources that I started to get confused. The messages got jumbled in my mind. So many spirits were coming through for different people. Finally, one night, my boss called my mother. She told her I was suffering from sleep deprivation, and was in no condition to drive. I knew nothing about the phone call, until I saw my mom. When I reached the car, I insisted she take me back to my apartment. When I arrived home, I noticed the board was now gone. It had slipped my mind that we had gotten rid of it, when a Bible was hurled across the living room. Could it be that my boss was right? Am I sleep deprived? I knew I wasn't sleeping, yet, I didn't feel tired. That night, I slept for 16 hours straight. When I woke up, I was late for work. I called my boss and she told me that I needed to take a couple of days off. I looked in a mirror and was shocked at what I saw. My reflection showed big, matted, tangles in my hair. What was going on?

Since my husband and I had broken up, I haven't been back to Thurber or used a board to communicate with the spirit children. Were the kids upset with me for not going back? Did they think that we had abandoned them? I was getting more confused. So many things that I couldn't't explain, not rationally anyway. I had no one to turn to, and nowhere to go. Every day there were signs, more Spirits communicating and reaching out from the beyond. Wanting something and the board was all I could think of to use to get answers. But I feared the board, more than what I feared what was going on around me. I needed to eliminate that thought out of my mind.

I didn't know what was happening to me and questioned if I was going crazy. I couldn't go into my bedroom- there was something dark in there. There was something nesting and growing stronger, watching and following me, making me do things that I didn't want to do. This entity kept attacking me repeatedly, night after night, lurking in the still of the darkness. I felt I was in a situation in which I had no control. I called on the angels for help. Were they listening? Help me! Please! I pleaded for their assistance.

The dark activities continued. The final step was during a bath. While soaking in the water, I felt a magnetic force in the water attach itself to my belly button ring. The magnetic force was slowly pulling me to the drain. I was terrified in my own bathroom! I decided to also close off that part of the apartment. I felt the evil that had come into my home, had a nesting place, and that the evil force was feeding a portal to hell.

Nightly, I communicated with the angels around me. Could they hear my cries, quietly in the back of my mind? Repeatedly through the nights of terror, I called out to them to save me.

As time went on, the activities increased. The blinds in my kitchen changed every time I walked in there. I kept straightening them throughout the day, but each time I walked into the kitchen, the blinds had changed again. I felt like it was a game Maria and her friends were playing. My bedroom, however, did not have the playful mood of the kitchen. Each time I entered into my bedroom, I felt like I was being watched. Something frightening that had been hidden in the depths of my mind. Shortly thereafter, I didn't go into my bedroom anymore.

While taking a shower in the 2nd bathroom, the feeling of been watched came over me again. While showering, I felt like something was near me, washing my hair. I repeatedly dropped the soap. Even with the shower curtains open, I was frightened to my core. I was living in fear, day after day, night after night. Were these fears founded in fact? Was I living this, or was this something I had created in the depths of my mind? Was I feeding these terrifying thoughts?

I felt my life was spinning out of control. I sensed it getting stronger, feeding off of my fears. As the terror grew, I was getting weaker. You could see major changes in me. I am a social person, yet I chose to live isolated from everyone . I abandoned all my friends, except for one. I met Matt on a dating site. We had been chatting for a while. Matt and I had many conversations about Wicca. I questioned the path I was on. Did I need to change my path? I am of British decent and Wicca was in my past, so it was easy for me to explore Wicca. Matt taught me about candles and how to use them, as well as crystals for protection. With these protective measures put in place, the odd activities in the apartment began settle down. I still only entered my bedroom if someone was with me. The feeling was very oppressive and my friends noticed that it was colder in that room than in the surrounding areas. Dark, damp with an evil energy to the place. He was waiting.

One night, at my job as house mom, I was upstairs in the two story building. The top floor was the dressing room for dancers. This room was huge and surrounded by mirrors. One night, one of the girls had given me her cell phone to hold while she went on stage. All the girls were downstairs performing or getting ready to go on stage. I was upstairs, alone, working. After her dance number, the dancer asked me for her phone. It wasn't where I had left it. It was gone! I told her to go back downstairs and I would continue to look for it. Upon finding it, I would bring it to her. I searched everywhere, but no luck! I finally discover the phone. The chairs in the dressing room are metal folding ones. I found the phone magnetized to the chair. Metal hair pins, that had fallen on the ground, were lining up, all directed towards where I was sitting. Metal curling irons did the same thing. This was scaring me! Was I being affected at work as well? It seemed that the odd activities in my apartment had settled down-and things were quiet on the home front. What was going on, now? Had this dark entity found me at work? In reflection, it made sense. A lot of the dancers were young mothers, addicted to the dancing industry. Drawn to the fast money, booze, and the nightlife. A lifestyle filled with adulation and the use of drugs! A path of self-destruction. A perfect place for evil to dwell! He had found me!

 One Saturday night, the club was festive with a party atmosphere. The club was filled with customers. I was upstairs, alone. I felt a heaviness in the air. I was startled to hear the sounds of footsteps coming towards me. Whatever had been lurking, was now making his entrance! He was getting closer, I heard a loud noise in front of me. I was terrified! The temperature dropped in the dressing room. Something had dented the metal lockers! At that point, I reached my breaking point. I ran down the stairs! Straight to my bosses office, I told him "I quit!!" I hugged the girls telling them I would be in touch, and made a quick exit. I never looked back!

In a conversation, my friend Matt had told me that when we had dabbled in the spiritual realms unprotected, a dark wizard had been unleashed! I was starting to wonder if this could be true. Was this the source of the haunting?

After leaving my job, I was now confined to my apartment. The next day, I called Matt in Atlanta. I explained to him what was happening to me and what had happened at work. I lost the connection on the house phone, so I called him back using my cell. Our phone conversation was repeatedly getting disconnected. I thought this was strange! The phone would repeatedly go straight back to the dial tone! I kept trying, but eventually, I was just getting a busy signal. I finally had no choice but to give up. That night, I fought going to sleep! I was terrified of what might be waiting for me if I closed my eyes. I turned on every light in my confined living area. I was lying on the couch crying! I repeatedly asked the angels to help me! I drifted off to sleep. I noticed that there was a new angel with my angel Christopher. Did I now have two angels? He shared with me, that he was also male, and that I would know him as Jonathan. He would take turns with Christopher watching over me! I always felt better when my angels were there. I would fall asleep in the arms of my angels. When I awakened in the morning, the lights and TV that I had left on, were now turned off, so I knew that someone besides myself had been there.

One day I came across my neighbor, Elizabeth. I hadn't seen her in a couple of months. She invited me over, and as I talked she listened. She is a single mother, raising her three year old daughter Katherine. We prayed together and she offered to come over and bless my home. She anointed my windows and doors with holy oil she kept in her kitchen cabinet. She told me to get the Lord's Prayer and hang it on my bedroom door.

As we continued throughout the house with our blessing, I had fears of going into the bedroom and bathroom that I had closed. I never entered those rooms anymore. It had been so long since I had been back there and I wasn't going freely! I was scared of what was lurking, manifesting, and feeding! The room was cold. The air was heavy. The bathroom was dark- a lot darker than what I had remembered! We said the Lord's Prayer rebuking whatever was in the room to leave. Elizabeth drew crosses in oil on the windows, mirrors and all doors. When we were finished with the house blessing, I felt better.

To continue with the spiritual cleansing of my home, I utilized some of the recommendations from a website called Demon Busters. I spent hours that night going through the sites pages! I then turned to the Bible. Psalms inspired me, and I read 92 out loud. I used the healing power of music. I filled the computer room with the Holy Spirit, playing only positive, spiritually uplifting music! Happily, I noticed the blessing techniques were working. I was feeling better! The evil entity was gone.

Over the next couple of days I had finally found some light in this dark cold tunnel. I had broken through my self-imposed isolation. I felt some relief and comfort. I felt I was not fighting this fight alone. I discovered other people who were going through similar situations. Elizabeth and I had become good friends. As we prayed together, I felt strengthened. I know that when two or more come to the Lord to pray, the prayers are stronger. I believed that! I also turned to my Bible for inspiration. Many times, I had picked up the Bible with the good intention of reading it, start to finish. Sadly, I could never get past the first chapter. Frustrated I would lay it down. I discovered a unique way to receive messages from the Bible. I would open the Bible to a random page, and whatever verse was there pertained to me.

I continued to fill the computer room with gospel music. My favorite CD's was Mercy Me. Each day, I was feeling better. I felt the entity was gone. I was slowly starting to let go of some of my fear, and started living my life again. I had friends over again. I had a friend that decided to stay with me for a few days. The house seemed peaceful. Would it last?

One night I was completely caught off my guard. I was alone, and a dark shadow chased me down the hall. As I ran into my bedroom, I made a huge error in judgment. An entity was waiting. I stopped in my tracks. The room was freezing cold. The air was so heavy, that it made it difficult to breathe. I jumped on my bed, hidden under the covers. At this point, I was crying hysterically, rocking, pleading, and begging "don't hurt me." I was looking around the room trying to figure out where "it" was. I could feel a strong presence, and the pictures in my room appeared to be changing, almost coming to life. I ran out the house that night! I started to pound on my neighbor's door, but I didn't want to wake up her daughter. In my frantic search for safe haven, I ran across the street to Wal-Mart. I had ran to the bright lights of the store when I was scared before. I got some water and headed to the closed snack bar area. I sat in the empty snack bar area and thought of my life. It was early morning hours, and everyone was home safe in their bed. I did not safe in my bed or safe in my home. Help me find my way of fighting back. I was a mess.

To calm my mind, I sang gospel songs, over and over in my head. This helped to calm me, but I knew that I had to do something. I couldn't continue on like this. That moment is when I decided to fight back. I decided it was time to get some help from a source that would help me find my way of fighting back. I knew of a shop off of Beach Street called the Emerald Forest. It is a metaphysical store that has a large variety of items. The store was busy and I wasn't comfortable talking to anyone about what was going on, so I spent a couple of hours there looking for something that resonated with me. I walked around holding the crystals, and checking out the oils. They had some stones in a dish at the checkout counter with different sayings on them, like

Protection, Peace, Love, etc. I wanted one so I picked

out Protection and headed back to the books. A lot of

them were Wicca, some were spiritual, inspirational,

and I found them comforting. As I continued browsing

through the store, I thought, this place is magical,

peaceful, and spiritual. At peace in the store, I realized I

wasn't afraid. I came across some black candles, but I

wasn't sure of the uses for them. I finally got the

courage to share my situation. I asked the clerk for some

advice. I explained the short version, and he listened

and believed me. He told me that black candles were

for binding and banishing negative spirits. He also

showed me the Hematite's, which are also used for

absorbing negative energy. Quartz crystals, oils, this

place was too good to be true! Finally, I had the

weapons I needed to fight back.

As I was checking out, I asked the clerk about what I

could wear that would keep me safe when returning

home. He handed me a Hematite on a chain. He rang

me up and wished me the best. I thought, " Yes, I am

going to need well wishes." I knew that this was a spiritual battle. This was my personal war to fight and I felt that I had prepared myself with the ammo needed, to do just that -fight for my life. I had been in despair for so long. I just wanted it over. One way or another it would be done. Heading back to my truck I thought of something else I wanted, the peace stone. After making my second purchase, I felt a peaceful energy come over me. I could be comfortable with that!

On the way home I thought of my plan of action. How was I going to handle this? I came up with a plan. I had confidence, I was ready, and he's going down. I prayed all the way home, asking the Lord, Goddess's, Angels, whoever was out there, for help and guidance. My prayers were answered. I received courage, strength, power, unconditional love and protection. I now had a plan; the computer room was the place to go, so I reviewed how I would unlock the door, and run straight through the house. My sanctuary was the computer room and all I had to do was get there. I knew that I would be protected, so I put on my shield of armor and could feel the angels were waiting.

As I summoned up the strength to enter the apartment, I asked for Archangel Michael's assistance. He is God's warrior and will always be there when you have a battle that needs to be fought. I had to make sure that I had my mind occupied on other things. I knew that the darkness would be observing my every move. I am not sure how, but I knew, I had to focus on the task at hand, and not to get distracted, but to keep going forward. I had faith that I was protected, and through that faith, I would get through this ordeal and survive. I prayed over my amulet, then I put it around my neck, together with the cross I already had on. As I entered the apartment, I immediately put on some music, my favorite song "Soul Shine" by the Allman Brothers. I have so much faith and comfort in that song, and I knew it could help me through this situation.

The apartment was cold. The foul energy had grown, and the darkness had now spread into the living room. I felt the gateway to hell was taking over most of the apartment. It seemed like the whole apartment was a porthole to a dimension I wouldn't want to visit. I got the black candles out and set them on the table along with the crystals. I had plenty of other candles from the many trips to Wal-Mart. I placed candles along the door way of the room, lighting every one of them. I prayed asking the Lord to forgive me for whatever I had done. I promised that if I got through this I would serve Him and dedicate my life to those being haunted. Whatever it took, I would do. I was so tired of dealing with this evil energy. I just wanted this to be over. I got some additional candles. I put them in a circle in the center of the room, and sat in the middle of it. Once inside, I slowly lit each one, and then placed the peace stone and myself inside the circle. I remember saying I was tired, but then my mind goes blank. I have no clue what happened next. When I woke up, I was lost. Was it over?

What had happened? I woke up in a fetal position. Time had passed without my knowledge. All I knew, was that it had been a long enough time period for the candles to burn out. I felt reborn. I was well rested and completely energized. I was still holding the peace stone in my hand. I did not remember picking it up. I looked at the stone and noticed there was something inside of the peace stone. It was an image of a man's face. The face had a goatee and was grey. I then noticed something else was trapped in the stone. An image of a demon gargoyle that used to sit on my roof and terrorize me. Somehow I had caught them! I did not know, how I had caught them, only that I had.

I found out later, the wizard had left his host around the time I was being terrorized. To my knowledge, he has not been seen again.

I eventually moved out of my apartment and to my mother's. I originally thought I had put this chapter of my life to bed. I was mistaken.

Several years had passed. One afternoon, a friend I called "the Lion," and I were in Fort Worth. We were getting things ready for a trip to California. The list was long, with I.D. renewals, shopping and other last minute errands. While completing our final errands, we found ourselves, near the apartment complex that I used to live in. I had passed this area many times, but had never had the courage to stop. Today was different. I had the strong feeling that I needed to stop that day. As we were driving near the apartments, I asked the Lion to pull the car over. Yes, it was one of those sudden unplanned stops.

I had the overwhelming feeling that I needed to make sure that there were no children trapped in the apartment, there had been so much activity during that time of my haunting. Something was pulling on me, calling out to me, reaching from the beyond, and I simply couldn't ignore the cries. The apartments have an electronic gate. Usually, to gain entrance, you must punch in a code. We pulled up to the front gate and it was standing open- inviting us back. My former apartment was in the first building near the entrance. I had no clue if my former neighbors still lived there. What would they think of my showing up? I saw my former neighbor, Elizabeth at her job in a local store from time to time. However, over 2 years had passed since I last saw her. I remembered how much support Elizabeth had given to me during the 5 months my apartment was taken over. I now consider her one of my angels. Elizabeth, along with my Michael, helped me with spiritual warfare. They assisted me in defeating the nasty evil that had waited for me in the darkness, five years ago, in my home. It was a sunny day and fairly warm, as we walked up to, what I hoped, was Elizabeth's apartment. There was a slight breeze, a typical, gorgeous, spring day in Texas. As we turned the corner to the building I could feel a lump in the back of my throat. Fear threatened to engulf me. I had vowed never to return, but, here I was. Stopping, I looked up at my old bedroom window. Before, when I looked at the window, I would sense a gargoyle, who would sit on top of my apartment roof and terrorize me. Instead, I found it was wide open- which scared me. I immediately got an uneasy feeling. I thought to myself, "what if they remembered me, could I be in grave danger?" Would the Lion be able to protect me? I could be in danger. Glancing over at what was once my computer room, I saw that the window was opened, however, everything was quiet, and there was no movement inside the rooms. I started to climb the stairs, and with each step my heart pounded, my pulse raced and my palms became sweaty. The nervous feeling in the pit of my stomach grew, as the fear was building up inside of me. But, I had to go forward, I had so many questions that needed answering. We had already come this far, might as well push through the fear and find out about the children. At the top of the stairs I stopped. I ran my hand over the door of my apartment, scanning for any energy that might be dwelling within.

I was curious about the current occupants. I was wondering if they experienced anything paranormal. While standing outside of my former home, I was searching for some small impression, a glimpse of evidence, a manifestation somewhere in that apartment. I wanted to warn them, tell them to get out, before it was too late, yet I was helpless. The Lion stayed at the foot of the stairs, watching my back. He provided the protection I needed so I could proceed forward. With him there, I knew I was protected and safe. I knocked on the door next to my former apartment, of what I hoped was still Elizabeth's apartment. Rustyann, her daughter answered the door. What a relief! Right away she remembered me. The Lion came up the stairs and we went into her apartment and visited for a while. She told us Elizabeth still lived there and she was helping a friend install carpet in a nearby apartment. Rustyann explained the apartment I lived in had been vacant for a year after I left, and only recently had been rented. My former apartment never returned back to normal after I fled. Rustyann told us that the apartment management had to completely redo the kitchen including the cabinets. She went on to tell us that you couldn't walk up the stairs for months after I had fled because of the Darkness. She explained that they still hear bumps in the night, activity in the computer room, walking by the apartment some nights, and noises coming out of the kitchen. While looking up to the window, glowing eyes were seen staring down at them, piercing in the intensity, cutting like a knife. Rustyann mentioned that the occupants never stayed the duration of their lease, something always drove them out.

Rustyann was relieved to see that I was doing well. This was the first time, we had seen each other or spoke, in five years. Funny how things change, yet, remain the same, frozen in time. She went on to say that her mom was talking about me a few nights ago, wondering how I was doing. On one level, I was relieved that Elizabeth wasn't home. I remember Rustyann looking at me one day and saying that I had gone over the edge, lost it, snapped. She went on to say how I had changed, "something wasn't right," and she thought I was possessed by something evil, dark, and demon like. I had been speaking in a language that I did not understand. After hearing me speak the strange language, Rustyann avoided me and went in the other direction when she saw me. We still had a few errands to get done, so before it got too late, we left. I hugged Rustyann and thanked her for her time. I left feeling things were different now. There was some closure and we both could move forward. As soon as I left her apartment, I could feel the heaviness descending. I could sense something wasn't right. Rustyann had told me that she and her mother had endured financial difficulties since I left. Other negative things happened in their lives and they couldn't seem to shake them. I felt that they needed to move, but with their financial situation, moving was not an option. As I walked away, I felt so helpless.

As I walked near my former front door, a part of me wanted to knock on the apartment door. I wanted to talk with the woman currently living there and try to warn her, but I did not. As I came upon the kitchen window, with its' blinds closed, I reached out my hand. The kitchen area was a major activity zone in the paranormal occurrences that had happened in that apartment. With my hand outstretched, I was immediately taken back to the time, when these blinds seemed to rearrange themselves, and I would keep bending them back into shape, day after day. I paused and slowly glanced up at the porch. A flood of memories poured forth. I was mentally being taken back to the nights of torment. I was afraid to go back into the apartment, to cross the threshold of hell. I remember the many nights, praying, begging, and pleading on that porch. Some nights, I was so scared, that I would attempt to lock out the demons. I would get on my knees, and scrap the brick, sealing, locking out, all demons that dwelled between the hours of midnight and 6 a.m. With clearer thinking, I now realized I was doing the opposite of what I should of been doing. I was sealing them in! Not sealing them out as I wanted. I had created a gathering place for the dead. There was so much darkness there, I was feeling overwhelmed, dizzy and feeling faint. I felt like I was being smothered with negative energy. Walking away, we could feel eyes watching our every move, trying to draw me back in. As we headed back to the car, I showed the Lion where the grass had burn marks with images of angels, and how the bricks had changed into the forms of spirit children.

These are the eyewitness accounts of the next events:

Sierra's account

I faced my fears that day going back to my apartment. I have always said on my radio shows that I wanted to go back and clear the apartment of all the negative residual energy that was left behind I had forgotten about this until today. These are the actual events that took place.

I went back, myself, Ama and my friend Lisa. We astral traveled back into my haunted apartment to close once and for this entire chapter in the book. I sent pictures to two of my team members, Marleys and Lisa. They could see things in my pictures that my guides said I was not ready to see. I wanted to know exactly what was going on to keep the others safe. I was indeed ready to face this head on it was time to do so.

Marleys was the first to email me back she told me that there were many negative spirits swarming around me in my computer room and she also had visions of skulls with flames and a heavy darkness. In the corner, to the right of me, the closet was the doorway for spirits going in and out, the portal. During my haunting, I thought the computer room was safe. I am now finding out that it was not. Something was growing in the pit of hell, night after night, breathing, I was so afraid of this happening. I had not heard back from Lisa. Later that night, I had logged into our spirit rescuers community chat on my networking site of Ning. I wanted to see if

Lisa or Ama was in the chat room, if I was to put closure on this, I needed the validation on what I was feeling and what I was up against. There was a reason I went back that day and revisited the apartment. The pieces of the puzzle were coming together. Lisa responded agreeing to astral travel into the apartment and wanted to take a look around see what she could find. There were a few of us in the chat room. We sat back and quietly listened to what Lisa had to say.

Lisa's account:

When you first sent me the pictures, I kept seeing darkness and glowing eyes. When I went into the house, I was greeted by a little old woman with blue gray hair. She was standing in the kitchen. She stated that she didn't like the new people, because they never put things back where they belonged, and she always has to keep looking to find them. Then she said, that they don't take care of things like they should, everything was neglected. As I started to turn, I saw a cat. It was gray and white and hissing while looking at the stairs leading up to the apartment. As I moved towards the steps, the little old woman warned me not to go into the bedroom. She said, "stay away it belongs to him." As I moved forward, I heard a growling coming from my right. Then I heard her once again telling me to be careful. Looking to the right, I saw a large, blue grey figure about eight feet tall. It almost looked like a gargoyle with wings. It was standing on the side at the bottom of the steps. Its eyes were glowing green. I didn't know what to think and it didn't say anything.

As I looked around, I saw a dark haired, younger man standing at the top of the stairs and when I looked into his eyes they were black. He put his head back and started to laugh. It was a scary laugh, it made the hair on the back of my neck stand up. I started to go up the stairs and he disappeared. I looked back, and the old woman was standing there and she told me "DO NOT GO UP THERE, he is evil!" As I turned and started back down, I could feel something watching me. The old woman said that he controls her because of her fears. Without the fear, there would be no hold. When I got to the bottom, the gargoyle growled again. The lady told me not to worry about the gargoyle. I said goodbye and left.

Later that night, I talked to Sierra on the chat, and we were validating what I had seen in the apartment. Then the old woman came to me, and told me, that she was part of Sierra's family. She was her Grandmother. She told me about her family. That was when she said that Sierra would have to go back, but there would be three. I knew one would be Sierra, one would be Lisa, but we did not know who the third one would be. All we knew was that it was a woman. As we were talking in the chat room, Ama came in and Sierra was telling her about what I had seen in the apartment. Then the old lady came back again, and was telling us things. That was all I remembered- there was so much going on.

Then Ama said I needed to take it back and face this head on. I was still talking to the old woman when she said "it is now." I (Lisa) was astrally, pulled back into the apartment just as I approached it. The old woman yelled "protection now." As I started to put up a white shield of protection, Sierra kicked in the door, planted both feet and threw a large sword straight at the man on the stairs. I saw the sword go into his chest and then he disappeared.

Sierra's account:

Ama was the next to come into chat. She said. "Sierra go in, take care of business, then get out" "keep it simple and don't look back, but face them and get rid of them." I was ready and angry as I grabbed my sword from Archangel Michael! I was looking dead into the demons eyes. With attitude and strength, I throw the sword never taking my eyes off of the demon. Once my sword struck him, he just disappeared right in front of me. It was over that simply. That direct- in and out. Listening to Ama and Lisa, I went in, got out and faced my fears, the demons from my past. I felt re-energized,

glorified, tough and relieved. Lisa now calls me her

Thor. One moment was all it took, to end five years of

torture that I lived. The weight was lifted off my

shoulders. Immediately, years of torment were gone.

The little old woman in the kitchen, that spoke to Lisa

with the British accent, was my grandmother, and she is

a conduit on rescuing earth bounds and is still with me

to this day. The man on the stairs was evil. His name

was Ron and he looked like Steve McQueen. He wore

blue jeans and a white collar shirt. He was the Incubus

that raped me, night after night, day after day. The cat

that Lisa saw was Maverick, she was a year old. Her fur

had patches of different colors; grey, white, and black.

During this ordeal, my furry friend, Maverick, supported

me. I believe that the horror of my haunting was too

much for her to handle. Many nights she was left

outside, on the stairs of my apartment. I was too afraid

to open the door during the "bewitching" hours. When I

fled my apartment, I gave her to Elizabeth. I could not

take her with me, and she died soon after my leaving. I have since then, gone back into the apartment and erased the residual energy that lingered there. I did this remotely without ever having to leave the comfort of my living room. I can move forward now, and continue with my promise to God. This was my journey and I survived it.

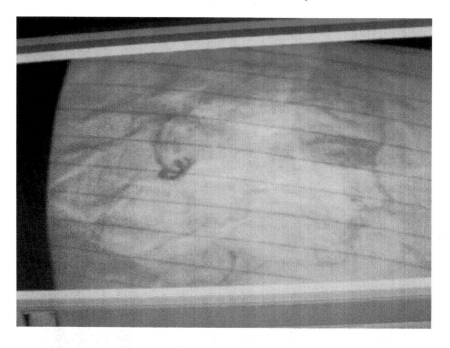

Sketch of my son Christopher was drawn in my apartment!

Jesse and Maverick -mist moving through the carpet

The beginning- arm coming out of my jacket

The Wizard in the stone (left side)

Chapter Two
New Hampshire

My first Spirit Rescue was in the town of Milford New Hampshire. I was there visiting friends for my 43rd birthday the summer of 2004. The houses in New Hampshire were simply breathtaking, built in the old Victorian Style. Joanne owned a 4 level Victorian home next door, which could have been mistaken for the plantation in the movie "Gone with the Wind". To bring in more modern flavor to her home, she had a tanning bed on the 4th floor. On the same property outside in the back and to the right, was a charming Little White Cottage, which had been converted into a Duplex. In the late 1700's the property was owned by a wealthy family and was then the servant's quarters. This is where I spent the 10 days I was there.

 Almost immediately I felt strange sensations entering my quarters. I felt heaviness, sadness, just an overwhelming, scary feeling for a first time rescuer. Little did I know!

The Duplex was divided into an upstairs and downstairs apartments, and I stayed in the upper level apartment.

The staircase, white in color, spiraled to the upper level, and it didn't matter if I was going up, or down, I always felt like eyes were watching me, or I was being followed. I couldn't shake this uneasy feeling that rippled through my mind and my body.

As I entered the apartment, I was immediately greeted by negative energy, my stomach felt like I had just been hit with a baseball bat, and someone was sucking my breath away, almost choking me. I knew that I wasn't alone. I left the apartment and went to explore the rest of the property. Down the stairs and out the door the heaviness had lifted somewhat. The property was peaceful, and while I was absorbing the surroundings, I realized that I was being shown the homes. As I check out the houses around me, I felt a sense of peace, not at all like I had previously experienced inside the house.

Each house had its own story to tell and in the attics, lingered spirits of children that were being held by something stronger. I knew then that I was brought here for a reason. The light within me shines like a beacon to the departed lost souls of children. The spirits knew that!! The next morning when I awoke, I felt well rested. I must have been tired from my flight. I slept through until morning which surprised me, for not once did I wake up during the night. This was surprising because just the night before I hadn't slept at all because of the spiritual activity going on at my apartment in Ft. Worth. I grabbed me a cup of coffee and headed for the shower. After refreshing myself with a shower and a hot cup of coffee, I ventured outside and noticed the temperature was a lot cooler.

 Down the street I noticed that someone was having a garage sale...At home before I confined myself to my apartment, I indulged at least once a week. I always said I needed a bumper sticker that read "I break for Yard Sales" and this one was huge. They had all kinds of things, antique dressers, old books, toys, clothes, antique knick-knacks, I was running my hand over some of the items the energy was amazing! I ended up picking out a musical wooden box from the early 1900's. I bought two figurines a little boy and a little girl of the same era. I realize now, years later that these things were tools that I needed in the Spirit Rescue. The final thing I purchased was a black leather backpack! To carry my things around during the time that I was here!

During my 10 day stay, I went to many of the local historical places. The Milford Oval had a lot of paranormal activity. The land was a gift from William Crosby, and his house was on the site of Town Hall. Standing there was The William Crosby Memorial, a World War 1 Monument marking the site of the first town meeting house.

The Bridge Settlers built bridges across the Skowhegan River, a pathway to cart grain to Shepherd's Mill. I could feel anger, sadness walking along the bridge. The bridge was built 1845 and it was the first made of stone. The previous three bridges were washed away because of flooding in the area.

In 1784, between two pine stumps, the residents of Southwest Parish of Amherst built a Meeting House, to avoid the inconvenient trip to the church in Amherst Village. They placed the meeting house on the west side of the oval. In honor of his friend the Rev. Humphrey Moore, Mr. Perkins Nichols had the Paul Revere Foundry cast a bell in 1802. He gave the bell to the Meeting House. The House was moved to the north end of the oval in 1837. This was when the town was no longer required to support the church. The house was raised to add a first floor to provide the space for two stores. The Post office and Library were in one of the store spaces for years. A basement was added later for fire equipment. For the price of Fifty-five dollars, 26 citizens subscribed to purchase a wooden eagle to place on top of the Town House. In 1869 when the present Town Hall was built the Paul Revere bell was moved to the New Town Hall. The Eagle remained and gave rise to the name Eagle Hall. Eagle Hall was moved to its present location on the northeast corner of the oval and it is owned by the IOOF and the first story is again used as a church.

 On the original 120 acres granted to John Sheppard, his son John Sheppard, Jr. built an imposing 2 story home for his wife Mercy Wilkins in 1757. This magnificent wooden structure stayed in the family for three generations. Brothers Steve and Charles Burns, who now own the home, opened the Colonel Sheppard Inn in 1992.

I spent a couple of afternoons in The Milford Library researching the history of this Township, going through birth and death records of the names of woman, children, and men. I was looking for validation little did I know that I found it. The library was built in the 1950's on the grounds of Lullwood Estate. The fountain is a memorial to Col. Oliver Lull; who perished serving our country in the Civil War. The new addition was opened in 1986. I remember the first time entering the library, although this is just a fading memory that lingers in the corner of my mind. As I climbed to the top of stairs; there was a Librarians Desk. She pointed me in the direction of the older part of the Library, where records were kept in the W. Lull History Room. Stepping inside and closing the door behind me, I realized this was a small room with a couple of cubicles. I quickly chose one of the cubicles and started gathering historical information about the township. Immediately I began pulling goodies out of my black leather bag. There were 2 women in the room; they were gathered at the long table reading a book. I later had a conversation with them and discovered they were searching for the history of a young boy, paranormally speaking. This room had a lot of history to it. Along the walls were old books. The energy in the room was peaceful but I could tell that we were not alone. I just had the feeling that this was a place of comfort. This was the place for numerous town records, and the original record book dated 1794. While researching I felt like I had been taken back to the 1800's, and what it was like living in their era.

The women wore turn of the century dresses, hat and umbrellas (used to keep the sun off of them). The men were dressed in their tailored suits with ascots and spats, with matching hats and socks, and the children were dressed down, not in there Sunday's best, but for playing and fishing. The bridge had a feel of heaviness, lives lost of those jumping off the bridge and fights, almost wanting to cry. In the Bales Elementary school a spirit walks the hall, upset over losing lives and changes, and there were far too many people and too many changes within this school. Over by the Gazebo, in the oval, a spirit of a man walks smoking his cigar known in the paranormal as a residue haunting over and over repeatedly. The family outside of one of the homes had several spirits where children use to run and play in the yard, while the maids where in the house working. In one of the nearby cemeteries some of the dead are not at rest. A person buried there that should not have been. I got the feeling that he had done something to one of the other guests.

The next day was my Birthday and decided to head over to the oval in the middle of the town of Milford. Walking us past a small cemetery I stopped dead in my tracks. There was a fence that went around it, small in stature and size. At that time I had only been in one Cemetery and it was in the town Thurber. I could hear them crying out for me to help! As we got closer to the oval you could see all the shops that were on the square. We headed to the Italian restaurant to eat lunch and after we had finished our lunch, we walked around the Oval. Taking in this picturesque area and thinking how peaceful this place was. The town's folk were very proud of the men that served in different eras. Each war had its own wall of names of all those who had lost their lives. They had benches and gardens to show honor and for all the visitors who would gaze upon the walls. You could tell that this was an important part of the Oval. Their memory continues to be cherished and not forgotten to this day.

I took off one day alone, I was drawn to this bar that was on the outskirt of the Oval, but the name escapes me. But walking in you could feel that the owner was proud of his bar. He had done all the woodwork himself and the care and craftsmanship showed in this little pub. It was small and hidden in the corner of the Oval...The barmaid handed me a beer and as I was standing at the bar talking to her when I felt someone push me. He told me not to get behind the bar I was standing in the waitress station at the end which had a wooden door you lifted up! I asked the woman if I could look around and take some pictures. This place was amazing, and as I turned too look, thinking it was the waiter, and there were three spirits that haunted this place. One was the original owner; one was the waitress who had worked there when it first opened and a woman who was a customer. The barmaid told me the story of the waitress and how she loved this place, and she was such a dedicated worker that even in death she would walk by the tables and look out the window. One of the rescues that I did was in the tiny apartment.

The Oval looked much different than during the day, there were so many turns on it almost like going through a maze and I got lost. Somehow I got turned around and I was walking down streets that didn't look familiar. Joanne was at work and the rest of my friends I couldn't reach on their cell phones either. I could feel myself starting to panic and I focused on the Harley's going around the Oval. To be honest there was a part of me that wished I was on the back of one. Then my cell phone rang, and I was given directions to the house. I knew it wasn't too far, walking earlier on I was so drawn to some of the houses I wasn't paying attention. I knew that I had to go back by the cemetery. As I walked up on the cemetery this time it was dark, with very little light. I had this gut feeling that I must not enter. No matter how much I wanted to, I sensed danger and uneasiness.

The other side of the street had more lights so I decided to cross. I was drawn to this big white Victorian House, someone or something was watching me from the window. The feeling wasn't an uneasy feeling. I went ahead and took a picture of the house When I developed the film, there was a spirit looking out the window, the silhouette was of a man peeking out. The middle window was an animal, a cat hunched up.

Finally reaching the house, darkness had settled in for the night, it was around 9 p.m. I went ahead and retired for the evening. Lying in bed I kept hearing a woman's voice calling out to me in the darkness of the night. I drifted off to sleep.

I woke the next morning early; I wanted to make one more trip to the Oval. This time was to a little Five and Dime store that had caught my attention a few days earlier. The first place that I was drawn to was these charms that you would attach to a bracelet. I wanted to get something for my daughter. There were several different charms to choose from; again I was led to purchase the following. An airplane, a little boy, a birthday cake, a cross, a sign that read I believe, a little girl, and the letters C, D and R

The message read as follows: (D) for Dakota, I took a trip by plane, (Charm) for my birthday along with me was my guardian angel the letter (C) for Christopher that was sent giving me guidance and direction. The little girl charm that was pink represented the girls I sent into the light. The Boy represented blue for the boys, (R) was for the receiver, Have faith cross (charm) I still have my charm bracelet to this day. Looking back now it was the best Birthday present I could have asked for. My first rescue " paranormally speaking."

I was getting messages from the house across the street from the spirit of a woman, her name was Mary Tooney, and she lived there during the turn of the century with her husband. She was building up my confidence. It was nice to know that I wasn't going crazy. Mary was channeling with such love and comfort. For the first time I wasn't afraid. I felt safe. She reassured me the angels were guiding on the upcoming rescue. The children in this cottage died during the same time frame, along with other area children that were left behind, trapped in the dark shadows of the unknown and mystery.

The house had a secret small room under the stairs. I had been too scared to look in there, but tonight I got up the courage and opened the door. A small confined room, 4 by 8, cold, damp foul, and had an odor to it. I heard sounds of children cries in the night when I was alone. The energy in the room was positive. Was this a balance? They needed to be reunited with their parents and loved ones waiting on the other side and to be embraced by the warmth of the light, to be safe in the loving arms of their parents.

I gathered the children that night setting them free. I lit a single white candle to help them on their way. There was peacefulness in the flame flickering with different colors of a rainbow. I grabbed the music box off the table winding it up, setting it on the floor in front of me.

I pulled the two figurines out of my leather back pack of the little boy and girl that I purchased at the garage sale a week ago. I was unsure of how to cross them over, but somehow I just knew I was being led, this was meant to be. I started with a prayer, asking my angels for guidance and understanding, needing their help with the transition. I felt completely humble as I was on my knees praying I was being guided.

I could feel the children's presence around me. I could also tell that there were more than what I had originally thought. The energy there was more than four. Almost immediately I began rocking. A small child had climbed and was sitting in my lap. Sitting there quietly seemed like an eternity. I could tell we were shielded in the loving light of the angels. The atmosphere suddenly changed. Bright light filled the room and I asked the children if they saw the angels? I knew that they did. How could they not?

I was feeling so much sadness, excitement, peace, and love. This was it, not sure what happened after that. I sat there I just sat there. I kept asking myself over and over if I had done the rescue correctly. How was I to know if they crossed safely? I was frozen almost statue still, waiting for the answers.

Almost jolted, I realized the atmosphere was lighter, like someone had turned on the sun. The single large dark cloud over this home was gone and had disappeared. I was being pulled, directed over to the window and I saw the entire neighborhood was shining.

 Exhausted I headed into the bedroom, feeling good about what just happened. As I got undressed and slid into bed I laid there, playing the rescue over in my head. I couldn't help but think I had played a small part in something bigger than I had ever imagined. I finally drifted off to sleep.

 This was my last day, my flight was leaving this afternoon and I was heading to the big D. I wasn't ready to go, wasn't ready for this adventure to be over with. I felt that there was so much more to do. I was just starting to feel safe and I was afraid to go back into my apartment. I knew what was waiting there. I was haunted by the Incubus and he let me know he was waiting lurking. Here I was finally at peace, I was sleeping at night. I wanted this to last. My neighbor Joanne allowed me to go through her house with my video camera. I was going to tan for the last time, and entered her house through the side door that led to the kitchen. Looking up at the ceiling the paint was peeling off and showing the original tin. I started in the living room and worked my way up the stairs. I was scared, and I could feel the hair on the back of my neck stand straight up. Joanne had gone off to work leaving me alone in the house.

The higher I climbed the more nervous I became. Reaching the third floor my heart began racing, something about the energy. I kept thinking this is where the ghosts tend to hang out. I was starting to get a knot in my throat finally reaching the fourth floor.

By this time I wasn't sure if I wanted to tan or not. Laying there for 20 minutes in confined space thinking about all this was more than what I could handle, me and the ghosts, no way. Sure I had tanned here a couple times already, but not like this. Not like going through the house alone I had literally scared myself.

I ended up giving into fear and got undressed. I pulled out the portable CD player listening to tunes. As I laid there under the florescent light tanning in the heat, I drifted. Trying to get into my zone, every once in a while I did pop open the lid to making sure I was still alone.

As I headed to the airport that afternoon I knew what was waiting for me back in Texas. I boarded the plane, I sat in my seat feeling stronger, more connected not so alone. I knew that I could call on my angels if needed. I also knew that I could call on Mrs. Tooney, the spirit of the woman that showed me the way.

The Old Cemetery on the way to the Oval Milford N.H.

Cemetery on the way to the oval.

Downtown Milford New Hampshire Mist to the right of me!

Standing on a bridge on the way to the oval face in the water.

Chapter Three
Pennsylvania

I moved into my mother's home in August of 2005. Fleeing from the apartment, I couldn't let go of what happened and what I went through. It was still haunting me in every aspect of my life. Even though I was safe at my mother's home, I decided to leave Texas behind me, forget the haunting, and move on. I did just that and found myself in Chambersburg Pennsylvania. I remembered the promise I had made to the angels, ask, believe with your heart that they are there, and they will be. Trust, my friends, that is all it takes.

Pennsylvania was beautiful. You could see the smoke coming off the top of the mountains in the early mornings, especially on cloudy days. My new home was located in Chambersburg. It was nice, 3 bedroom, fairly new, brick house, deep in the outback of the mountains. My favorite place to relax was on the back porch. I would often sit out there, drinking coffee, with a notebook and pen. My roommate had a nice wooden patio with ivy plants placed all around the rail. Covered in the corner, a BBQ grill was used to cook hamburgers and hotdogs in the coolness of the summers evening for family and friends. Wooden benches set the mood. I had found my serenity, my eternal peace, a new beginning.

I was beginning to get back in touch with nature, as I felt especially connected to the trees. The lovely sounds of birds chirping, whispered quietly in my ears. On the ground, there were acorns everywhere, the leaves were turning orange and the squirrels were gathering the acorns, preparing for the upcoming for winter. I sat back, sipping my coffee, very aware of my surroundings. I needed to unwind my mind and spirit, take time out. I was looking forward to spending the winter here. I wanted to experience the making of a snow angel, something that I haven't done since I left the winters in England as a child.

I had made a couple trips to town. Lot of old stores, with a history wanting to be told, and a bookstore ready for me to explore. There were dirt roads, leading into corn fields, giving you the feeling of the "Children of the Corn" movies back in the early 80's. A lifestyle very different from what I was used to. I found it a little scary. Although the area could be creepy, the people were so interesting! The Amish lived in a life style that seemed like you had stepped through the doorway into the past, a portal taking you back in time. Everything was so simple. It was evident that they appreciated hard work, and the simpler things in life. I remember the first time I saw a horse and buggy on a small country road. It stood out from the passing cars. I thought that the mixing of the different times on the same road was so cool. Their carriage was a deep, black with a pearl shine. You could tell that they took pride in their wheels. Literally, one horse power!

Pennsylvania has many paranormally active cemeteries. A large number of lives ended during Civil War battles and the graves of the fallen are spread across the state. The Sollenburger Grave intrigued me every time we went through town. I wanted to stop. Chambersburg was one of the many towns that were wiped out during the battle of Gettysburg. This was a paranormal battle field that was rebuilt on after the war. So many young soldiers lost their lives. Armies of young boys fought and died here. The energies associated with their violent passing still exists. I had served in the Military, so could relate to the soldiers and understood the sacrifice these young soldiers had made. We use to unwind at the American Legion post in Chambersburg, a place we would go to shoot pool, watching NASCAR on a Sunday afternoon; it is one of my fondest memories looking back. I was in Chambersburg only two months.

Next, I moved to the Village of Pleasant Hall. This was a very small community. The house that we lived in was 200 years old. Through the years, the various owners had done some renovations. A major renovation occurred in the early 1900's. We lived next door to the Pleasant Hall Fire Station. Every once in a while, you could hear the sound of sirens. Every New Year's Eve, they would toot the horn to bring in the new year. The houses that surrounded ours were old. Many still in their original style. Seeing them took me back to my trip to New Hampshire. I had my own P.O Box and would take a short, pleasant stroll every day to the post office. I didn't feel comfortable with mail coming to the house. I wanted to leave no trace of my location. I was afraid that the spirits/incubus from my former house would find me. I wanted no part of that!

One sunny day, I decided to take a walk to the cemetery. It was a Saturday afternoon. Lots of leaves on the ground, with a crispness to the air, a sign that fall was here. I figured it would take me about 10 minutes to get there. I had my portable CD player, so I took a walk. As I walked, I couldn't explain it, but I could feel the fear building up inside of me. I pushed it back down and put it out of my mind. At my destination, there was an old church and behind the building, a small cemetery. This area was not closed off at all like the one at Thurber, I noticed there was a lot of loved ones here, families, you could feel the energies were light and positive. I wasn't scared of my surroundings. I walked around, checking out the headstones. Some were dated back in the 1800's, and I felt connected to that era. Was that time period one of my past lives? I had been reading about them on the internet. You could see that there were a lot of young children buried here. I lost track of the time. It started to get dark and I realized I had spent 3 hours there. As I was walking back to the house, I was feeling so peaceful. I had a great afternoon. I was alone in a cemetery in a hero township.

Questions kept flooding my thoughts. I desperately needed answers to them, so I joined a couple of online, paranormal groups. One of them was The Paranormal Research Society. That is where I met Valerie; she is the founder of the group. She posted some valuable information. I had never been in a yahoo group before and I was inexperienced on the computer, so this was going to be a challenge. I was lurking in the group, sitting back, reading every email that came through. I couldn't believe that people were talking about their paranormal experiences. No one was judging. Everyone seemed knowledgeable, and it was awesome they knew what they were talking about! One afternoon, a couple of weeks after I joined, I decided to tell my story. I had no clue where to start, so I just started typing. I wasn't sure how the group would take it, but I knew that I had to talk about my haunting. It was so hard retelling the story of my nightmare. The telling brought back so many of the fears and emotions. This was one of the hardest things I had to do, I couldn't get past the attacks, but I had to do something to get closure. I had to heal. I knew that I was safe so I proceeded to share. When I was finished writing about my encounter, I hesitated before sending the message out. Taking a deep breath, I pushed send. I was curious, were they going to run with what I had said? Think I was crazy? I nervously waited. Emails started flooding my inbox.

They listened with compassion, as if they were feeling my pain. They knew where I was coming from. Finally, someone really understood. The members were letting me know that I wasn't alone, this was happening more and more. In the paranormal phenomenon world, I finally had support, people that I could talk to freely, and that felt good. I realized then, that millions of individuals turn to the internet for help. As a result of the acceptance, I now co-own the Paranormal Research Society with some awesome people. Our group has approximately 4500 members.

On a Sunday afternoon, late in November, with snow still on the ground from Thanksgiving, I was spending time with my friend, Crystal, and her boyfriend Joseph. It felt so good to be among friends doing fun activities. We decided we would do some cleaning and rearranging of the house, to prepare to decorate for Christmas. Crystal's daughter, Tatum, was spending the day with her Grandmother. They usually went to church together, and after services, the Grandmother would bring her home. The holiday season was approaching, and today we wanted to surprise Tatum with the decorating of the family Christmas tree. Crystal's house was old, but the rooms rocked. I appreciated the history of the house and the aura essence. We were boxing knick-knacks up and were going to pull decorations for the house out of the attic. The attic had been intriguing me for some time. I first noticed the attic door when I was in Tatum's bathroom. I noticed when I was alone in her bathroom, by the door, I would see in the floor tiles, the face of a little boy. I was seeing him more and more, but had decided to just ignore it. As we entered the bathroom, Joseph opened the attic door. I have always been fascinated with what people keep up there. I finally got my chance to check out the attic! The attic was darker, cooler, damp and spooky. An old sewing machine sat in the corner, boxes filled with NASCAR treasures. I thought back to the attics in New Hampshire, spirits hung out in cool dark places (negative ones). I wondered how many were here. Looking around there are a lot of different things in boxes that had been stored and forgotten. Crystal told me that there was a Ouija board in one of the boxes. It has been stored away for years. She told me how she use to play with the board as a teenager when they had slumber parties. Crystal offered to find the board so we could play with it. I declined. I wasn't going to provoke any spirit that might have come through the board. Kind of like a "been there done that attitude," and I wanted no part of it! I told Crystal I would start bringing out the boxes, while Joseph was looking for the Christmas tree.

A few days later, I was bored one afternoon, so I thought I would go back to the cemetery up the road. There was snow on the ground from the previous night. I wanted to take some pictures of some of the headstones that were there. I needed to get away and clear my head for a while. When I got home that night, we noticed something in one of the photos. There was a clear outline of a spirit in the snow. It appeared to be a small child. The child was a little boy, and he told me his name was Tyler. Was this the little boy whose images I kept seeing in the tiles of the bathroom floor?

Something told me that it was him. I started hearing his cries for help. Almost like a child was whimpering. Every time I heard the sounds, my hair on the back of my neck would stand on ends. I noticed that it always cold in my room, too. Were these signaling another encounter? Was this a beginning? I hoped not since, I was doing so well adjusting to my life in Pa.

I received the message that Tyler was 10 years old. I kept telling him that he needed to go back to the cemetery. That he shouldn't have followed me home; I didn't understand why he was around me. I kept hearing Tyler crying, what could I do? I jumped on the internet and asked for some advice. I scrolled through some of my previous emails. Could it be that I needed to help him cross over? I had done this before, but did I do it right? The only thing I knew was to pray. During my prayers, one of my online friends instant messaged me. Her name was Joyce, and she was a Wicca mother. She said that she would assist me into crossing him over. I agreed. With Joyce assisting me, Tyler did go home that night. But what I didn't know was that there were more around me.

Chambersburg was having their annual ice sculpting exhibition. Texas does not get cold enough for those kind of events, and I really wanted to check it out. The exhibition was in the old part of Chambersburg. Close to the old book store. A perfect time for me to check out some history culture in this township. We parked the car, dropped quarters into the meter and headed to see the first ice statue. The ice sculptures were displayed in front of each store. Some had started to melt , but I could see that there was a pair of doves, a squirrel, a dolphin, a bear and other animals. After checking out the sculptures, I walked into the old book store. As you opened the door, the little bell rang. I was greeted by an older gentleman who was standing near a small desk. The air was thick with the smell of old books and their mildew. I asked the man where I could find the paranormal section. He pointed me to the far part of the store marked New Age. It was a very small section and the name was crazy to me. What is up with that name? I would say that paranormal is anything but new. Hauntings have been going on for many years. I looked through some of the books that were there, running my fingers over them, the energy was strong, almost electrifying. I could feel someone was behind me, I knew that it wasn't Tyler, because, we had sent him to the light. Who could this be? Then I felt a soft nudge, like I was gently being pushed. I asked who was there, but I received no answer. I continued to look around the store. They had old record albums, a replica of the Declaration of Independence, old pictures, lots of ancient history books. I went back to the New Age Section. I found a psychic book written by John Edwards, and I ended up purchasing it. I always loved watching his shows. I also came across a Hans Christian Anderson book of fairy tales. I loved his stories as a child. This particular volume was dated 1904. It is so old you can't open the pages, but to me it is still a treasure. My favorite, of his fairy tales is Thumbelina. A lot of Hans

Christian Anderson stories are still in print around the world. His stories are in book form and also have been made into movies. His writing has been brought laughter and joy to little faces for many years. Hans stories have been enjoyed by generations of children. My daughter's favorite was the Little Mermaid.

Christmas came and went, and odd things were going on in Crystal's house. I remember one night the area above us flooded, and the ceiling almost came down on us. The lights would flicker, and alarm clocks were messed with, making us late for work on more than one occasion. Objects were starting to disappear. When I was alone, I always felt like someone was with me. I was too scared to use the board to find out what was in the attic, so I decided to make a pendulum. An online friend, Valerie, had posted directions for making a pendulum to the group. I thought that would be an easy way of asking questions, with a simple yes and no answers. The pendulum required an old dangly earring,(I think every woman has one of them lying around), and a chain. Gathering these 2 things was super easy for me. The directions said that I was to wear it for 8 hours to charge it with my energy. To me that made a lot of sense. The following morning, I sat on the front porch enjoying my coffee outside, it was a nice day. I grab the camera, and as I sat in the swing, I again had the feeling like I was being watched. I wasn't scared this time. The energy was different from what I had previously felt. I was more experienced. I had successfully helped some souls to cross over. I also knew that I had friends on the internet if I needed them. I was ready. I took a long drag off my cigarette, then stomped it out, I reached for my camera, without taking my eyes off of the house. I asked my guides to lead me, show me, and shot some pictures. I was using a Kodak digital camera. Easy to use and share. We could upload pictures to the internet, something I was getting good at. Looking at the pictures, we noticed, in the top right hand window, something was looking out. I shared the photo with some psychic friends and asked what they saw. They all came back with the same answer- a woman.

Over at Mystic Investigations, I knew of a Medium named Anna. Occasionally she would be online and give readings. I signed into chat, and then got in a line to ask her a question. This was the first time I had ever done this. But I needed to know who the woman was in the house that watched me. I was second in line, and I multi-tasked while I waited. Finally, she asked if I was in the room still, I replied yes! Anna started to go into a trance. She picked up on my energy, and had me join my energy with her. We both focused on my question the we both channeled a woman and the name Melba came through. She was at the house with 3 other woman, but it was Melba that had a message. Melba told me that I reminded her of her best friend that had lived in that house many years ago. She considered me an old maid at the age of 43. Her best friends name was Kathy. She was married and suffered mental abuse from her husband. I found out that the flowers I had been drawing were from her, she loved flowers. Crystal's front yard had flowers every spring. Melba is 35 years old and she appears at the window when I am outside. I would always talk to my favorite Deity, Apollo, while smoking a cigarette and swinging. She says we watch each other. I know that she is there, but I wanted to make sure this was a positive entity, especially with what I had been through. Another realization dawned on me in the chat room.. I had another gift- it was channeling. This gift went hand in hand with my automatic writings. I thanked Anna for her help. We have emailed each other a couple of time since that message from Melba.

The next morning to say "Hi" to Melba, I put some flowers outside. As it was winter, they were the fake ones. It was winter in Pa.- it was not the season for planting. I told Melba they were for her and that I hope that she enjoys them. A friend was not happy that I was pursuing a friendship with Melba. My friend told that it wasn't healthy for me or Melba. Melba needed to go to the light and she needed to know that I wasn't her best friend. I had never done a rescue like that before. I went ahead with what my friend suggested. She told me to sit somewhere quietly and call the person. Once she came looking for me, I needed to take her home. To prepare to help Melba, I went to the front porch and called on Apollo for guidance. I always loved the warmth of the morning sun. I helped Melba to cross over and I never heard from her again. Melba meant me no harm, I know that. In my heart, I know that she went into a healing place with her friend Kathy, and will someday be back. I know she is completely at peace.

Soon, I was working at a local Clothing Company. Crystal had worked there for 5 years. She told me that they were hiring and got me on out there. This was a big factory. That made Trousers, Tuxes, uniforms, etc. and my job was to do pocket flaps that were on the inside of the pant leg. I had never worked with a sewing machine and wasn't sure I could do it. I was eager to learn something new and challenging. I noticed my life was finally coming together. I was finding myself again and that was a great feeling. The factory was a long tin building, at least over 50 years old. There was a section in the building that would be much colder when I would walk through it. I later found out that it was an electro-magnetic area. We were on a Lay line. I never questioned that area again.

To stay busy, I ended up joining a gym that was located by Letter Kenny Air Force Base. In one of my online groups, I started chatting with a guy name Justin. Justin lived in Texas. His Great-Great Grandfather was buried close to the Letter Kenny gym I exercised at. It was called the Rock Springs Cemetery. I told Justin that I was close to Letter Kenny and that I work out 3 times a week, so I would check out the cemetery and shoot some pictures, then send them out to him. He wanted me to shoot some pictures of the inside of the Church, his grandfather's headstone and grave. Through emails, Justin told me that his Great-Great Grandfather's name was John Burns. The cemetery was a prerevolutionary graveyard dating back to the late 1700's. This fascinated me. I was learning that Pennsylvania had a lot of history to offer paranormally speaking. The next time we were at the cemetery, I spent some time walking on the grounds picking up different energies. The energy varied, depending on where I was at the time. The first thing I noticed was the big numbers on the front of the church 1794. Rocky Springs Church was organized in 1742 by the reformed Presbyterian Church forty years later. The Majority became part of the Associated Reformed Church in 1802. The name then changes from Rocky Springs to Conocheague, dissolving the congregation in 1898. The church stood alone. Untouched with boards on the windows. You could tell it had been that way for some time. Behind the church, stood the little cemetery, no Historical Marker, no grounds keeper, just a small outhouse to the side. We searched all over the cemetery for John Burn's headstone but the cemetery was old and the names were no longer visible. I asked my guides to show me the area where he might be resting. I was still learning. I shot some pictures. Jumped back into my vehicle and drove off. I wanted to send the photos to Justin and gather more information, before I continued. Two weeks later, I returned. I was determined to find John Burns.

I wanted to give Justin the photos he had requested as a special gift to remember, his Great-Great Grandfather, for John Burns' memory needed to be honored, he was a hero.

John Burns was a God honoring, truly remarkable man. He emigrated from Scotland in 1747. It was John Burns, a patriot, who by using a hammer, forged the first cannon in America. He served in the ranks as an Officer in the army of George Washington. He took a wife, Ester Morrow. They left Adams County, PA. in 1773 and built their beautiful home on the banks of the Antietam Creek. This thrifty Scot started a business. He had owned a saw mill and a blacksmith shop, even though he had no tools for casting metal objects. After the decision was made, to make a cannon, for the Patriot Army, John worked relentlessly to complete the task at hand. The women also banned together and made steaming hot meals for all that helped so that they could complete this endeavor. After John had prepared the core, his neighbors heated iron bars to whiteness, then he then removed them from the bed of coals, and welded them to the core. His hammer had never rang so true. It rang all the way to the Hills, echoing back. This penetrated the dark with a ring that could be heard for miles. With the tools that he had, such that they were, he fashioned a bore for the cannon, and it was smooth and round. It was not a monster cannon, but when the primer was applied to it in the Battle of Brandywine in 1777, it had deadly accuracy. The cannon was captured there by the British. From there it was taken to the Tower of London and it is there to this day.

This was my last trip to the cemetery, I had allowed enough time to find him, he deserved to know that he was loved, and his family was proud of the achievements, he had made in the world. This time when walking through the gate, I asked permission first, "may I enter?" In response, the energy was peaceful, a slice of heaven. I could sense there was no turmoil, and no anger, no frustrations, the spirits were happy. This was their final resting place. You could feel it. There was peace in this valley. I asked John's spirit to meet me at the gate. Jumping out of the car, I was anxious, determined! John would guide me to where he was buried. I was feeling confident. I felt someone gently touching my hand, leading past numerous headstones, through several areas of the cemetery, until finally we stopped. We had found the grave. I was sure of it. I had looked at this headstone on my previous trip, even stopped and read it. It was one that I couldn't read, Today I was seeing it for the first time. In very faint letters, you could make out the name John. He was close to the front of the cemetery, but there was no recognition, no flags, and no trace that a hero was buried here. I sat on the grass, praying silently, thanking

John for all he had done. I let him know he made a difference and had touched other people's lives through our history. I told him about his Grandson, and how I believed John Burns was Justin's Hero. This cemetery was a legend in its own time. One Grandson finally got peace through some pictures from me.

I ended up staying one more month in Pa, as I continued to learn about my gifts. There was one more place I wanted to check out while in Pennsylvania, so I moved into a small trailer on the foot of the mountain, just outside of Pleasant Hall. The population was almost none. There was a cemetery right down the street about 800 yards from the house. You could see the headstones glowing at night. I felt the spirits all around me. I could feel them in the yard, also in the trailer. I did a lot of walking while I was there. While in Pennsylvania I didn't drive. Walking seemed to be a good way for me to clear my head, think about things past and present. I found keeping my mind centered was an important tool to moving on. On the night of the full moon, I remember grabbing my camera. It was a clear night, june bugs were hitting the windows, attracted to the light inside. I snapped a couple of pictures of the moon. Not sure why, but I walked to the cemetery that night. The church in front of the cemetery reminded me of the school house on "Little House on the Prairie", Laura Ingalls was my hero. I loved the bond she had with her Pa, unconditional love. The grass was freshly cut, they used a riding lawn mower, and I could see it parked by the church. Looking through the windows, it seemed like there had not been any recent activity. I never saw any cars the month I lived there. The small gate that went around the grave yard was the only way in. It was always unlocked. Exploring the cemetery, I was led to a headstone of a woman. She had passed away a couple years prior from natural causes. I didn't feel like it was a traumatic death.

However, I did feel like she had somehow lost her way. You could sense her there. When I looked at the pictures, her grave stood out from the others. I could see a flash of light with a greenish, glow- a signal letting me know she was there. Every time I look at the picture, I think of the nights spent alone at the base of the mountain. Near the small cemetery. It was now time to head back to Texas. I had grown spiritually in the nine months I was in Pennsylvania. I felt in my heart, I could finally go home to Texas and confront the problems there. I left with a better understanding, and I was feeling confident that I was heading down the right road.

I would consider Pennsylvania a gold mine for ghost hunters. If you ever in the area of Gettysburg, please take the time to take the tour. That is one thing that I regret. I wish I had been able to pay my respects to those young men that lost their lives in the Civil War.

Top window Mrs. Melba Pa

The headstone of the American hero John Burns.

Shooting Orb at cemetery by the little trailer

Chapter Four

Alaska

I arrived in Alaska, the day after Mother's Day, May 11, 2007. The flight to Alaska was a long one and I had a 2 hour layover in Seattle. After my wait, I jumped back onto Alaska Airlines and headed for Anchorage. The excitement was growing! Growing up, I had always heard that Alaska was beautiful, with the mountains, the snow and of course, the Northern Lights! I was living out my parents dreams. I was eager to explore my new surroundings and meet new friends.

Our flight finally touched down, after twelve hours of travel. I arrived at midnight. It was just starting to get dark, and I was amazed, because, I had never been anywhere that it is still light at midnight. Anchorage airport was very big, and as I headed to the baggage claim, I had no clue where I was heading to, or the best way to get there, so I simply followed the crowd. I was text messaging my friend that was meeting me at the airport. As I stepped outside the airport, I noticed that the air was chilly, but the atmosphere was lighter. That morning in Texas, it was already starting to peak into the nineties, so this drastic change in weather was nice indeed! I remember sitting in the car, as we were heading to the condo, taking everything in. It started to get warmer in the vehicle. The heater wasn't on, but my butt was getting warmer. I told Steve I felt like I was on fire, asking him where the heat was coming from. He laughed and told me that the seat had a heater in it. I thought that was practical since the winters were harsh here.

When we finally arrived at the house, it was darker than when I landed, the mountains barely visible. We parked downstairs in the garage. The garage was used for a smoking area. We went through the garage, up the stairs and into the condo. The condo was huge! The house had a very big, living room with a corner fireplace, a nice size kitchen, three bedrooms and two baths. We all sat around and chatted for a few minutes, then I was shown to my room. It was 1:30 in the morning, and I was tired, yet, I was also excited to be in Alaska. I remember as I drifted off to sleep, it was starting to become lighter outside. The following morning, I woke up to the aroma of coffee. I jumped out of bed and headed to the kitchen, still extremely tired. As we sat down to eat breakfast, Steve asked me if I wanted to do some sightseeing later this afternoon, as he had to go into work till noon. He didn't tell me where we were heading as I walked outside the condo, I just remember the chill in the air. As I looked around, you could see the snow on top of the mountains, and everything was green, not like in Texas, where everything is brown from the heat of the summer. This place magically came to life; it was just breath taking, like living in a dream world. I headed to the shower and was anxious about the afternoon. It was still cold outside when Steve came home. He told me that I needed to bundle up, because we were going over the pass into Seward, which is a fishing village that was 200 miles away. I ran back in the house and grabbed a pair of jeans, putting them on under my leather pants, 2 shirts and 2 pair of socks. I also was wearing my black leather jacket, gloves and hat. In Alaska they have a helmet law where the rider has to wear a helmet, something I wasn't very excited about.

As he cranked up the Harley, the roar filled up the garage, and remember thinking "I love the sound of a hog." I was excited about this trip. We packed a change of clothes and Steve told me it is very cold at night here in Alaska so you need to be prepared if stranded on the pass. The ride was breathtaking, it was a beautiful day and the sun was shining. We rode for about 45 minutes and finally stopped at the local tavern to enjoy a cup of hot cocoa. We shot a couple games of pool as we warmed up. We had about 150 miles to go and Steve reminded me the sights would be beautiful, but the temperatures would be very cold. As we mounted the Harley and headed into the pass, everywhere you looked, you were surrounded by mountains and the ocean. This was a once in a lifetime ride, and we were making it happen. We stopped here and there along the pass shooting pictures, stopping to smoke and take in the scenery. The small town of Seward was a fishing

village. It was getting late, so we decided to go

ahead spend the night, enjoy the day here tomorrow

and then head back before it got dark. I had forgotten

for a minute this in Alaska it doesn't get dark. Sounded

like a plan, nothing paranormal was going on. For once

in a very longtime, I actually felt normal. We checked

into the Holiday Inn Express in Seward. We were tired

and hungry from the ride, so we decided to grab

something to eat. I can't remember the name of the

restaurant where we ate at, however, I do remember

what I ate that night Clam Chowder. I wanted to try

something new, an Alaskan dish. The clam chowder was

the best, and with that, I had steak and shrimp. We sat

there, by the window talking, there was no moonlight

reflecting off the horizon, but the night was still very

magical. As we walked back to the hotel, we stopped in

the harbor checking out the fishing boats, this was a

scene etched forever in the back of my mind.

The following morning, we walked around the village. It was early, and you could hear the sound of seagulls. Men were working on their boats, while others were cleaning fish from their morning catch. Boats were heading out and in, my own serenity spot.

We checked out of the hotel room, and took our time heading back to Anchorage. The ride was awesome! This time, we stopped to eat, before entering the other side of the pass. We stopped at a little log cabin for lunch; no one was there so service was prompt, and it had a nice aroma walking through the door, the smell of down home cooking. We took off our gear and ordered something to drink. I remember looking at the menu, and wanting something to warm me up. It was a lot cooler, today and the sky was overcast. We were expecting rain later this afternoon, still with a lot of miles to cover. I asked the waitress what she recommended, and she said, the clam chowder. This time, I had it inside a homemade bread bowl. It was extremely tasty, and I knew it would help keep me warm on the ride back.

As we left, I remember looking back, taking a picture in my mind. I wanted to remember every detail of this trip. The Harley started sputtering, as we climbed the mountains back to Anchorage. The Harley was a duel tank. We pulled over onto the shoulder. Steve told me, that we were running out of gas, but he thought that we had enough to make it back. He was worried. You could tell by the sound in his voice, with the added stress, that it was getting late. He told me there were no gas stations going through the pass, and if we were to get stuck, this was not a good place to be.

We sat there on the side of the road, Anchorage still 100 miles away. A man pulled over, to see if we needed help. We explained we were out of gas. Luckily, he had some in the back of his truck. He said he always carried gasoline for just this type of emergency. When we finally pulled in the garage, I was frozen and tired. I wanted nothing more than to crawl in my bed, and that is exactly what I did.

While I was in Anchorage, I had access to a computer and was able to keep up with our Paranormal Group. Some believe with all their heart and soul that we come into each other's lives for a reason, but we don't always know the reasons why. Enixer joined the Paranormal Research Society like everyone else, searching for answers to things happening in her life. Enixer put a plea into the group, asking for help on a blog, she had read. The blog discussed about a woman who was pregnant. She was a young mother, on her own and was feeling she didn't have the support of her boyfriend. She went on to share some of her deepest fears and concerns in the blog. Even naming her unborn child was discussed. I was convinced that Enixer heard her cries for help. This woman was on the verge of suicide and desperately needed someone . Enixer went on to explain that the woman wanted to keep her child, but felt she couldn't. Her final entries posted that she had made the decision to terminate the pregnancy and described what she was feeling about that course of action.

I was online, and saw the plea come through the group. I didn't know Enixer on a personal level; I did however feel a connection to her and wanted to help. Enixer told me she couldn't stop crying and felt she was at a complete sense of loss. She felt as if she was going through all the emotions and physical pain this young lady was enduring. To me this made a lot of sense, she had the traits of an empath, feeling all emotions in a situation. I jumped into action, and made contact with this distraught young lady. By seeing her through Enixer's eyes, we were able to connect with her. We literally saved this girls spirit. The woman was so overwhelmed by the love shown to her, that she posted day after day about it in her blog. She felt she had been touched and visited by an angel, and I believe she was. I was also forever touched by an earth angel, Enixer! She and I became more than just friends after this, we became soul sisters.

I have chatted with Enixer a few times since that day; she is very gifted and coming into her own. Our bond was very strong. Enixer had a vision of the two of us, represented in an image that came to her, of an angel and a dove. She told me that the image was for me. At the time, she didn't know what that meant. I was heading to Fairbanks and she was convinced it had something to do with that. When we have visions, we are only shown parts of the picture, through life lessons, we see all of it. We were talking about my trip and my calling to go. I knew that I was heading to Fairbanks for a reason, the bartending job there was just a small piece of the picture.

Through my internet messenger, Enixer buzzed me, she said that she knew what the vision meant and she was excited. Enixer is very talented with graphics and does all the artwork on my spirit rescue site. Her artistic talents show that she was touched by an angel, I would say. Looking at the picture she made for me, brought tears of joy to my eyes. The image gave me such validation as a healer. I needed this encouragement to move forward with my spirit rescue in Fairbanks. The image from Enixer showed a little girl (me) onstage, sitting at a grand piano, preparing for the performance of her life. She is playing an angelic melody, a song of flight to those that were listening, a never ending melody for the lost. A single snow white dove hovers over her, the dove representing the spirits heading home into the light. The music lifts the veil which had blocked them from continuing on their journey into healing, releasing them for their final destination home. In flight, the spirits were supported by the angels; embracing those lost, guiding and loving them each step of the way. I told Enixer that I wanted to see what the vision pertained to and asked her to write something. She did and this is what she wrote. I feel this is an Angelic message? You decide.

"You're Innocence is like a child; you are being transformed, into a Dove in flight. The Dove will soon take the transformation of an Eagle. The Gold ring. I see him grasping, will be the circle of life's changes. Don't fear! He will guide you and keep you safe. He is with many. When the light hits the gold ring, another soul will be lifted. He will drop the ring and swoop down to grasp it, one more time in a different area of the ring. Be safe and always remember. The Eagle is with you to guide you."

Enixer took it one step further. She made her vision into a graphic image for me and I made a copy. I framed it, knowing that I could go forward, safely on my travels, in the arms of my angels.

I had a morning flight into Fairbanks, and I was to meet my new boss at the airport. I had never met him and had only exchanged a few pictures. One thing, after another happened. Heading to the airport, I was excited, but also sad, I was leaving my friends. Steve had an uneasy feeling about this trip. He asked me not to go, but I felt like I couldn't stay. Not only was this a once in a lifetime opportunity of bartending in Alaska, I wanted to do this. I felt I needed to go. I was being pulled with a state of urgency. No one was going to talk me out of it, my mind was made up. I was flying into unknown territory alone, but I was okay with that. It was part of the adventure. Pulling into the airport, Steve helped me with my luggage. I had 2 bags on wheels and my black leather back pack I was to carry on the plane.

Anchorage has a pretty big airport, and as we headed to Alaskan Airlines, I was in luck, there was no line. Walking up to the ticket counter, I was thinking, "this was going to be a breeze," I handed the attendant my identification card, necessary for checking in. Steve and I were standing there talking when we saw my ID flip out of the agents hand, bounced off of her badge and hit the ground, or so we thought. It seemed to have vanished into thin air, nowhere to be found- poof, disappeared, and gone. She was shocked; she told me that in the twenty years she was employed with the airlines that had never happened. I told Steve it was paranormal.

The agent looked all over the place for my ID but it wasn't anywhere to be found. She then called security. They dismantled the ticket counter along with the baggage belt. I began to panic. It was getting close to time to board, and I had to make that flight!

They never found my ID, and after searching for 45 minutes. I was getting upset and wondered if this could be a warning. The ticket agent took me to the front of the security line. I was searched and let through, running all the way to my gate. I called Enixer and told her what had happened and she begged me not to board the plane. I told her not to worry, I would be in touch. I turned off my cell, as passengers boarded the plane. My seat was in the back near the galley. I asked the steward if I could have a Bud Light once we were in the air. The flight was only an hour long to Fairbanks, meaning there would be a very quick beverage service. When I finally got my beer, I had 10 minutes to drink it. With such a short flight, I had no time to be nervous, no time to worry. I was there and although it seemed like it took forever, finally the line to get off the plane was moving.

I followed the crowd to baggage claim. There stood this man in the background. He was leaning against a pillar, hands in his pockets, laid back- my new boss, Hayden. We loaded my luggage and headed to my new home.

The Alaska Gold Camp was amazing! The view alone was breath taking! No mountains, warmer climate, nothing like Anchorage at all, in fact, it reminded me a lot of Texas. The temperature changed drastically. Here it was close to the 80's.

The camp had just been bought by new owners. Upon my arrival, they were not open for business. Hayden was in the middle of hiring the staff. Getting things ready, planting flowers and other landscaping being done, the last minute details to set the perfect scene.

He took me through the doors of The Alaska Gold Camp.

The Gold Camp had been restored to its natural beauty.

A staircase led to the upstairs, the second floor had

been converted into guest rooms. The decor gave you

the feeling of the mining area, simple, but elegant in

their own nature and style. To my left, was a glass case

displaying articles, money, simple little treasures of the

mining industry. Hayden took me through the stained

glass doors which took us into the dining room, with a

bar to the right, that runs along the wall to the back of

the room. Through the swinging door was the

kitchen. Upon entering the room, I was greeted by a

spirit named Mark, he went on to tell me that he was in

the corner sitting at the table playing chess. I

acknowledged him and continued listening to Hayden's

tour. There were two glass doors on the right that led to

the patio overlooking the camp. I thought to myself,

"What a beautiful view, you could see for miles."

 Hayden told me that customers would sit out there

enjoying their dinner. He also said there was no smoking anywhere on the property, but on the patio old coffee cans placed on the benches to be filled with cigarette butts. Hayden told me that a careless smoker could send this camp quickly up in flames.

The view was a slice of heaven, very peaceful. I met the other employees that were hired on. Together we sat down and discussed the Grand Opening. We had less than a week. I was hired as the night bartender because of my previous work experience. Tourist season booms this time of year, and we were expecting a good season. A lot of tourists would be traveling to the camp. The previous owners had a respectable reputation. There was a lot that rested on Hayden's shoulders.

The next morning. I woke up eager and excited to start my day. We spent a lot of time cleaning the bar, scrubbing floors, stocking beer, polishing every piece of wood in the place to a glossy shine, and by suppertime, I was exhausted. I know I washed every glass behind the bar at least twice. I just wanted to relax with a cold beer. I walked up the hill to the cabins. I was told you could see the northern lights, from up here. The log cabins use to be Japanese huts overlooking the camp.

The only downside to the area was that unfortunately my cell phone didn't have a signal out here, so I was out of touch with my family and friends. That worried me. In the entry hall they did have a pay phone you could use, if you have a calling card, but I did not have one.

The following day, I met the girlfriend of my boss; this was when things began to change. The locals here were different; everyone knew each other and were suspicious of new comers, not like friendly Texas. They had their own way of life. Their lifestyle in an environment with such extremes created survivors. My first impression of Jackie was she was a jealous, insecure young woman, no parenting skills, so no respect for children and no respect for her elders, either. She was in a failing relationship with no way out. My cabin was next door to my boss'. I could hear all the arguments, the fighting and the accusations. I was beginning to think I had made the wrong decision. I thought I should have stayed in Anchorage with my friends, and that Enixer was right with the warnings.

The following morning I woke up to a knock on my door, it was Lizzie the waitress, she stopped by to tell me that Hayden wanted to see me in the office. I hurriedly got dressed and headed to the main building. I was nervous knocking on his door, but I went in and sat down. My prayers had been answered. He told me that his kids were coming for the summer. He wanted to give them the cabin next to his. Picking anywhere in the camp, I immediately picked the bunk house. I had wanted to go in there and check it out, but it had been off limits to all until that day. As employees, we were able to stay at the camp and the rent payments would be coming out of our first checks. Most of the employees lived in little houses renovated to their taste. The houses were all over the place, very close to the bar and restaurant. I could feel family of the upper management staying in them. I thanked my boss, closing the door behind me. I couldn't believe this! I was moving into the bunkhouse! I was so excited.

I left Hayden's office and went by the restaurant. I heard some movement in the restaurant, and after checking the doors, I found they were unlocked. Ashytn, the head chef, was in there drinking coffee and quietly eating her breakfast. Coffee sounded great. She asked if I was hungry, and offered to whip me up something to eat, and I agreed. While she was preparing my breakfast, I went behind the bar and poured a cup of coffee. You could feel the energy vibration was different. I believed it to be the ghost of an old woman; she has been known to walk through the bar asking about the children, 2 little boys and a girl. Even in spirit, she wanted to make sure they were alright. Some of the locals told me that she use to bake muffins and hand them out to the workers. I figured it was her way to say, "Good Morning. " From the chess set displayed, on the table in the back of the room, I could feel the spirit Mark watching me, not a bad feeling. but I knew he was there. I was not sure if the patrons would sit there and play chess, but the spirits I knew did. I usually set my laptop up in that area on my breaks, and I would do some writing. Standing behind the bar, I couldn't break my focus. I finally walked over there with a piece of paper and my pen. I kept hearing Mark very clearly in my ear. I pulled one of the chairs out and had a seat. I cleared my mind and I started to channel Mark. Without any thought on my part, I started to write on the paper. Mark wrote that he was one of the miners. He had seen a lot of different things over the years. I knew he was talking about the changes that had been made, but also a lot remained the same. Through my mind, he proceeded to show me pictures on the wall of some of the workers, their way of life, a proud union of brothers working the mines. Taking my hand he put it on his picture. He was nice looking I thought, a slender man, tall, dark hair cut short, you could see the hard labor over the years had worn on him, many hard hours of working in the camp. Ashtyn brought my breakfast over to the table and I asked her if she felt anything paranormal in here. She didn't answer me but the look on her face said enough. I told Mark that we had to continue this later; I had some packing to do. I wanted to go check out my quarters in the bunk house.

I entered the bunkhouse. As you walk in the door, you smell that old, closed up place, stench in the air. To my right were the stairs leading to the rooms. I went in to the first room on the left and was immediately greeted; I could feel the energy change. No one had used the bunkhouse in a while, but a couple of drifters had come through, from time to time. The previous owners had used it, but I didn't know what for. I just knew this place had a story to tell and I was going to tell it. I locked the bunkhouse up and started the climb up the hill to my current quarters to start packing. I wanted to get some packing done before I started my shift. Lizzie told me that she would help me move my things with her car, so I didn't have to make the walk. Today was slow, but a couple of the regulars came in to check out the new bartender. Ashtyn would come in on occasion and keep me company. I didn't think the day would ever end. I stayed busy helping Lizzie, assisting as much as I could with the tables, and our guests. During my breaks, I would run up to my room and eagerly pack another box. I wanted to have my things ready by the time we got off work. I knew we would be tired and I wanted to load it up, and get the move done. This was going to be my first night in this amazing place, and I was ready. I wanted to check the bunkhouse out in greater detail, with no worries of being interrupted by the living.

It didn't take us very long to pack up Lizzie's car. I only had the two suitcases and a backpack. We unloaded the car and I thanked Lizzie for her help. I went straight up to my room to unpack and get settled. I had a busy schedule ahead. I was working the next 5 days straight. My room at the top of the stairs had its own view, a small window looking back at the bar and the hotel. I could feel that I wasn't alone; someone was in the room with me. I didn't have a bad feeling, you have to remember that this place housed 100 miners so many years before me. The energy was different. I knew that it wasn't Mark. This energy was much lighter, calmer and it welcomed me. I asked who was there. I sensed a woman, a soothing energy. I sensed the spirit, was friendly, compassionate, and nurturing. I believe it was the old woman from the bar. I sat on my bed listening, she told me about a man. A local Judge named Jonathan Link, he had died two years earlier. I could feel him, standing beside me in my bedroom. His widow's portrait hangs behind the bar. I could feel the loneliness and sadness of the widow as I eventually drifted off to sleep.

My room was almost set up the way I wanted it. An old electric typewriter was found in my room. I set up a desk in front of the little window, making a personal space for working on my automatic writing skills. I was learning to communicate more with the woman from the bar. I knew she would be back. I would talk to Mark when we were alone. My bosses were always out

running errands, usually picking up supplies that we

needed. Occasionally, Hayden would jump on his Harley

to clear his head, and take off for a ride, leaving us.

Today was one of those days. Mark came through

again, this time he told me that he was born in 1921,

was hired at the age of 14 to work in the mines. He died

in an accident from an injury to the head, he was 35

years old. He seemed quite happy. He told me that he

took to me so quickly, because he could sense what I

did. I knew that I had been brought here for a reason,

but I still did not know exactly what the reason was. We

had Mondays off, as the weekends were the busiest. I

was aware that the bunkhouse was active with

paranormal activity, but I hadn't had the time to check

out the other rooms on my floor. In the still of the

night, I knew I wasn't alone, I could hear whispering

outside my room. Hayden told me I could set up the

bunkhouse anyway I wanted, as he wasn't planning on

opening it for a while. It had its own private kitchen

table where six plates and dinner utensils were laid out. I had no hot water in the bunkhouse, so I had to heat the water in the microwave. I had a coffee pot and a hot plate for cooking, and I took sponge baths, roughing it. I served twelve years in the military, so I didn't mind living life roughing it with the locals. I was working hard and having a blast. I stayed to myself, now retreating back to my room after my shifts. Tonight, I could hear footsteps moving up and down the hallway. The activity was awesome, and it was an interesting encounter, I did not feel afraid. The spirits had welcomed me with open arms and I knew my purpose. Little did I know. The boss's girlfriend and Lizzie were plotting against me...

The bunkhouse was home to 100 miners during the early 1900's. I am being shown madams leading men into the rooms. I have come to learn, that the spirits would come in and out of my room, some sit on my bed, some peek in and visit at my door. Enjoying my company, accepting me, allowing me to share their home, I was totally in tune with the residing spirits.

Tonight, they were taking me on a ghostly tour it seemed. The bunkhouse had rooms running down the hallway, on the left and the right. I knew the living didn't roam the halls as there was no laughter, no running, and no sounds.

As I begun walking down the hallway, I glanced into each of the rooms, some of them had posters of animals, whales, seals, etc. Walking down the dark corridor, I was feeling sadness, my heart was crying out. I was lead to the last room on the left, the only room that adjoined another. The family that had lived in the rooms, had separated the two rooms by a hanging curtain. The area I was presently in, was the children's room. There were two old, wooden bunk beds on each side of the room, and a small nightstand with a lamp missing it's shade. Walking into the parents room, I saw an unmade queen size bed, a dresser that had fallen apart with missing draws, and an old, worn out, wooden desk in the corner. Above the dresser, I noticed a paper posted to the wall. It was an old laminated newspaper clipping. When my eyes fell on the clipping, I got physically pushed. It wasn't hard, just a nudge wanting me to sit down, pay attention and telling me to read the article. In my mind, I kept hearing the sounds of a small child, a little girl. I began to read. The date of the newspaper article was August 16th 1935. The headline was in big letters: "Stricken by an Earthquake and Tidal Disaster." As I was reading my heart sank, many had lost their lives. There was so much devastation. There had been no warning notification and so little time to escape the pending disaster. The clipping continued to say that the areas of South Central Anchorage, Seward, Valdez and Kodiak were stricken. I thought to myself, "all these places are familiar to me, could this be a sign?" I took a moment to reflect on my travels since coming to Alaska. I spent the first two weeks in Anchorage, my second day, I took a 200 mile ride up the coast to Seward spending the night. Last night, I just so happen to have a cell phone signal, receiving a phone call from Steve. He had just finished a ride from Valdez and Kodiak.

I had never read about the earthquake and tidal wave. I started sobbing, not sure why I was crying, because I felt at peace. I was hearing the lost souls, reaching out for help, I understood that they needed to heal. I knew I was the one that could help to set them free. Now, all of this made perfect sense to me. Over 100 people had died, they was calling this the worst disaster ever in this area. The U.S. President had declared a state of emergency. In Anchorage, you can still see the crack running downtown, a constant reminder of the wrath of nature. I realized the scene had been set for another spirit rescue. I decided to help those spirits at that moment. We weren't allowed to keep candles in the rooms, as the bunkhouse was a fire hazard. I risked getting in trouble with my boss, but I lit a white candle that night. That candle represented peace, love and harmony. I burned it for only one hundred and eleven minutes. As the candle burned, I felt the spirits crossing over to the light. I considered if I had completed the rescue and I was wondering if the same little one was still with me. I was feeling the energy of a little girl, her name is Mattie. She is a very shy 4 years old. I asked her for a sign, to let me know, if she was still there. Mattie led me to my Grandson's picture. I had it on my wall next to the photos of my daughters. As I walked down the corridors to my room, you could hear the sound of my radio playing. As I got closer, I recognized a familiar song playing on the radio, "I Swear," my daughter and her father's favorite song. I was receiving the validation I had asked for.

Mattie then showed me her outline. I was trying to figure out how old she was, and she then allowed my hand to run all over her frail body. I was feeling Mattie, she was so tiny, and I was shown in detail her facial features, eyes, mouth, nose and ears. I now had a mental picture of her in my mind. She took my hand in hers, and settled down in my lap, I began rocking her, singing, and stroking her hair. Showing her a mother's love and making her feel safe. I sat there weeping softly, at one with her spirit. I called on the angels to take her to paradise that night, opening up Heaven's porthole, the last leg of her journey. Mattie was going home, and I sent her into healing. There was no nudging, no forcing, no arguments, she was ready, but she just needed my assistance. My help, finally helped her to finding peace in the light. I closed up the porthole, and thanked the angels. I sat on my bed, crying. I was very emotional, feeling the love of this child. I glanced over at my clock, the time 7:40 p.m. June 4th 2007. The radio was playing a new song, Sarah McLaughlin's, "In the arms of the Angels", I fly away from here, a dark, cold hotel room, was all that I remembered, as I drifted off to sleep.

The next day, I didn't want to get out of bed. I felt good about what had happened in the bunk house the previous night. I had a friend coming in this afternoon from Anchorage, arriving on the evening train. He was staying the weekend. Hayden told me I could set up a room for my guest in the bunkhouse with me. I decided to fix up the room across the hallway, and I wanted to make it cozy. I pulled one of the beds from one of the other rooms, dragging it down the hallway. In the hotel, above the bar and restaurant we had a laundry room, nice Jacuzzi area, and a bathroom available to the staff. I looked for some matching sheets and pillows cases. I went back to the children's room and grabbed the lamp. I made some final touches by sweeping and mopping, I had the room looking better than mine!

Almost time for work, Hayden and his girlfriend Jackie had left for the evening, heading to a nearby lodge a mile away. I was relieved they were gone, I was always walking on egg shells when they were around. Business was slow that evening. We didn't have much of a dinner crowd. Ashtyn and I spent some time outside, talking, smoking and discussing the problems we had with our boss. My friend finally arrived, and I showed him to his room in the bunkhouse and headed back to the work at the bar. Ashtyn asked me if we were eating dinner I told her yes. She reminded me that the last food order goes in at 8:30. We had no customers left. I was standing behind the bar, talking to Ashtyn's boyfriend, Lou and I was getting a burning, sensation in my chest, not evil, but I could feel the energy of the people that had lived here. They had lived a hard, rough life. I could sense arguments, bar fights and drunken customers. I excused myself, walking over to the chess set and sitting down. I could feel Mark behind me. I knew it was him, but the energy seemed different, there was a sadness. He told me that he was protecting me, watching over me. He loves when I walk into the bar, he says I brighten up the place, and I always acknowledged him. My energy was good, not like the negative energy of the living. The camp holds a lot of wonderful memories of hardworking men who worked together. The times were hard, but rewarding, and I was reminded of that by Mark. I felt like he was saying goodbye to me. Ashtyn told me she was closing up shop, and that she was tired. She left my friend Tom and I talking at the bar.

I can't remember if she told me to close the back door, or not, but what happens next shocked me. When my boss walked in, I could tell that they had been drinking, at the lodge, most of the afternoon and into the evening. They were fighting again. Hayden had a strong odor of booze and was screaming at the top of his lungs, upset that someone had left the back door open. He went into a rage! He called me from behind the bar that night and fired me on the spot. His reason? For leaving the door open; he also thought that some liquor was missing, stating he had marked the bottle. I never saw him check any bottle when he got back. He told me to pack my things and get out NOW, and I was to leave his property. I had nowhere to go, my cell didn't work, I had no identification and it was now ten o'clock, I was devastated.

Caught off guard and totally unprepared for what had just happened; I packed what I could, but I had to leave most of my things there. Fortunately, I had some money saved from my tips. I said goodbye to my new friends, the spirits that walk the halls, I could feel their sadness as I walked out the door, heading back to the bar. I had forgotten my purse and I wasn't leaving without it!

Sitting at the bar was Jackie, and Hayden, my former boss drinking out of the bottle I was accused of drinking from. I left that night on foot. I was so angry, I felt I was set up and the spirits were trying to tell me that. I just didn't listen; I had no clue in which direction to go. All I knew was Fairbanks was 27 miles up the road. Alaska has places you can go called Hostels. Hostels are very basic lodging for those that are stuck in Alaska for various reasons, accommodating them for a small fee. In other words helping the stranded, I knew I would be safe if I could get there.

A car pulled up behind me, and I had no clue who it was. My first thought was that it was Tom, maybe he was looking for me, but to my surprise Ashtyn had sent her boyfriend Lou to find me. If nothing else, he could take me to the Hostel. He was in as much shock as what I was. As we talked about what happened, our shock at what had happened-no one saw it coming! He told me that he had a house, that was condemned from having a lot of water damage, no electricity, the place was a mess, but I could stay there for a day or two. I thought at least that would be a roof over my head. I trusted Ashtyn and Lou, her boyfriend, so I decided to take him up on his offer.

Everything he said about the house was true. It was now Sierra's disaster area. But, I was thankful I wasn't on the side of the road anymore. I was safe and that was a start. There was an old bed in one of the rooms, so I put my stuff in the corner, sat down looking around, I couldn't believe this was happening. I checked my cell phone for reception, I finally had a signal, and day light was on my side. I cried most of the night in disbelief of what had happened, I was in shock. I woke up hoping this was a dream; little did I know I was in the middle of a nightmare.

I couldn't decide who to call. I didn't want to call my mom, she was worried enough. I didn't want to call Steve, either. I had to call someone, so I called home. As my mom answered her cell phone, I felt such relief !

Overwhelmed ,I started to cry. I knew she needed to know the truth and I needed to talk about it. I explained to her what happened. I assured her I was safe. I would find a way home, not to worry. I could hear it in her voice, my mom was very frightened, her only daughter lost in the Alaskan wilderness with only a bag of M & M's and 2 small cans of mandarin oranges. After my conversation with my mother, I deciding to call Steve. While dialing, I realized something, I had found out the meaning of Earth Angels on this trip, I had found two of mine. Steve and Enixer, both, came to me, in my time of need. Steve had only one thing on his mind, he wanted my safe return back in Anchorage. He assured me, I would be back at the condo by the end of the evening!

Passing time, I went off to explore the house. It was a mess! It looked like they had suddenly picked up and left. Scavengers had rumpled through their belongings. There were broken toys and notebook paper thrown all over the rooms, a sickening display of graffiti on most of the walls. I went outside, as I wanted to see where I was. Looking around the neighborhood, I realized that I was lost, and in trouble. I sat on the front steps, quietly praying for a miracle. The house gave me the creeps. The abandoned setting, spooked me. It was like re-living an episode of the Twilight Zone. During my whole month in Alaska, I had not seen any starry nights, and my days and nights seemed to run together. I had no perception of time, no beginning or ending of each day. I lay on the bed, under my jacket waiting for the cell to ring. It didn't. I was cold, tired and hungry. I never gave up hope, but exhausted, I drifted back to sleep.

The next thing, I remember, I was waking up to a woman standing over me. She was screaming at the top of her lungs, asking who I was and where did I come from, what I was doing there? I didn't know her, she didn't know me and I told her I was a friend of Lou's and he was letting me crash here. Not sure if she believed me or not. I couldn't help thinking, she would call the police and I was heading to jail, I had no proof of who I was. I had gone through so much, what was going to happen next? Lou told me last night, he would be back to check on me, I hoped that would be soon. This was late afternoon. I didn't have to worry about the sun going down for a few more hours. Finally, Lou pulled up in the driveway. I was relieved. I told him about the woman, he apologized explaining she was his best friend. She was checking on the house for him, while he stayed with Ashtyn at the camp.

Within minutes, the phone finally rang, it was Steve. He explained what was going on. He had spent an hour on the phone with Alaskan Airlines. They agreed to fly me to Anchorage. He told me the flight was leaving in an hour, giving me the information I needed to be able to board the plane, and he told me not to worry. I cried. I couldn't believe that through all of this, I would be ok. I realized now, that I am protected, in the arms of my angels. The airport was

15 minutes away, I had 45 minutes to get my ticket, make it through security and board the plane. Lou had managed to get my final paycheck ,and I thanked him. I

made it to the airport! While waiting to board my plane, I replayed the events in my head . I was so blessed that Lou was at the house when Steve called. Right place, right time! I arrived in Anchorage hour and 45 minutes later, safely on the ground. I was so happy to see a friend. As I walked in to Steve's, Sandy was still up. She looked at me and said "you amaze me girl." I hugged Steve, thanked him and headed to my room. I took a shower and fell into bed, falling sound asleep.

I woke up the next morning, Sandy's son, Carl, was watching cartoons. I cherished the sweet sound of his beautiful voice. He is Sandy's only son, a pure joy. Although mentally challenged, missing his 18 chromosomes, he radiate light of hope and courage. I knew that I was going to miss him. I spent that morning playing with him; he touched my heart, as did his mother, Sandy. She faced these challenges of raising a special needs child, climbing above whatever obstacles came her way. A wonderful mother, with her love and together, they will overcome anything life presents to them. She embraces her son with a love only a mother would understand. Sandy forever left a mark in my life, we still talk occasionally. Steve called me from the office, asking me if I wanted to stay through my birthday, allowing me to fly home on the 11th of June. What could I say; I wanted to get out of Alaska wanting nothing more but to go home. But through his kindness I decided to stay. He took me on one more ride up the coast June 10th 2007. He showed me the sleeping lady. I told him he was my Earth Angel, doing everything he could to make sure that I returned home safely, which I did. In that month I had grown spiritually and mentally, getting ready for whatever the angels had next. Forever changed through my Earth Angels.

My Birthday in Anchorage.

Enixer's vision of what Mattie looked like.

The Beautiful Graphics that Enixer made me!

Taking it all in!

The Entry way from the Bunkhouse!

Little boy sitting to the right of the headstone

Chapter Five:

A collection of short Spirit Rescues

Circle T Bar

The Circle T bar is a dark, hole-in-the wall type of place, located in the basement of a building. The place was damp, cold, and dark. It had an unpleasant smell of musk mixed with urine. In other words, your typical red neck dive. They have regular customers, that frequent during Happy Hour. The regulars are joined by newcomers, as a larger crowd gathers, for Karaoke on Saturday nights. This was the second time my friends had wanted to go there. It was early evening. A handful of people were sitting at the bar, an older couple was standing at the jukebox, looking for the perfect song to dance to. We walked up to the bar and ordered our drinks. Bones pulled a couple of quarters out of his pocket and began to rack the pool balls. Shooting pool was one of the things we both enjoyed and were both very good at. The rest of our group, Melissa and Higgins, were sitting at the bar.

While I was shooting pool, I felt the sensations of someone pulling on the back of my shirt. That had happened before when a spirit was trying to get my attention. I was learning how to shut down my gifts, so I ignored the tugging and proceeded with the game. I had lost, so I had joined Melissa at the bar. We were sitting there talking. Melissa looked down at the floor and was surprised to see a big puddle next to my bar stool. We got the Bartender, Simone's, attention and asked for a cleaning rag. She asked if we had spilt a drink. We said, "No there a puddle down here."

She replied with, "That is weird." She had never seen that before. She seemed receptive to anything, so I told her that I have a man in spirit form behind me. He was trying to get my attention. He explained to me that he's a beer drinker and a regular here and that this was his bar. She looked at me calmly, showing no alarm by what I had just told her. Simone told us that a man named Max had died 3 weeks before that. She told us she would be right back. Heading to the back of the bar and into the office, she handed me his obituary. As I read it, Max had died in his early 40s. I was sitting in his favorite bar stool. He had died from a heart attack while at the bar, after playing a round of golf. Simone had a pink stone shape of a heart that she carried around, it was a rose quartz gem stone. I asked her if I could hold it. Putting it into my hand, it turned red immediately, it was a sign for her. As it turns out, Simone was his favorite bartender. He was hanging out in the bar, but no one knew that he was there.

I called on the Archangels to guide Max into the light that night. He had a message for Simone and she luckily received it. The message was that even in death, love never fades.

Looking back, a lot of people have their favorite bar, I do as well. Many people come in to hang out during the afternoon, coming in for a couple of drinks before they head home for the night. Max was one of those folks. It seems natural for a spirit to head back to the bar, their favorite hangout, so they reconnect with great friends, great conversations, great music and booze.

Thanks, Max

The Local Coffee House

8:15 p.m. tonight I was actually on a date, it was a beautiful night, and the drive to Dallas was relaxing, not too many people on the road, no worries about traffic. My date and I ate dinner at a popular Asian restaurant in the West Village, It was the first time for me to eat Sushi. I was going through a growing phase. I was trying new things, not only in food but I had also been trying different new beers since I came back from Alaska. I was partial to Alaskan Pale and couldn't find any brews I liked better.

The restaurant was a small, quiet place. The hostess greeted us then sat us in one of the empty booths. Like on cue, a spirit was pulling and pushing on me trying to get my attention. I was on a date, so I ignored it at first. My date was explaining the different things on the menu to me, nothing really sounded good, but I finally made my choice. As we sat facing each other in the booth, talking, I started moving uncontrollably from side to side and then a quick sudden jerk. Ignoring the spirit was no longer an option, so I decided to ask the spirit what it wanted.

I am glad I took the time to reach out. The spirit was of a small child, a little boy around the age of 3 or 4. I explained to my date what was going on. He already knew I am a Spirit Rescuer, so it was fine with him. I continued asking questions. Suddenly, the little boy jumped into my lap and I immediately starting rocking, the energy was good and he was happy little boy. He had been trapped in the restaurant for quite a while. He was very excited to finally encounter a person with my abilities. He sat on my lap for the rest of our dinner.

When it was time to leave I asked him if he was ready to go into the light, he said no, my gut instinct told me to let him tag along with us, as I usually do, with the children. I have found that the children they seem to find peace with me. Upon leaving the restaurant I told him to take my hand. He was so excited to be leaving.

Tonight, I was prepared. I took my paranormal notebook with me, to show my date what I do. We decided to go over to Highland Park for coffee at a local coffee shop. As we walked through the door, he led me straight over to the teddy bears. We bought one for the little boy. While drinking our coffee, he was again in my lap, rocking and hugging the bear, you could pick up the bear and feel the weight was much heavier when the child was with it.

The lady that waited on us behind the counter came over and said they were closing. We finished our coffee, outside at the tables. Before I left the house, I had put the story of the children of Thurber in my notebook. I quietly called upon the angels to get ready. I then asked the little boy if he wanted to hear the story. He said yes. When I was finished, I asked him if he could see the angels. He said yes, and I told him that they were here to take him home.

My favorite part of working with children is to send them into healing and connecting them with family members waiting on the other side. I always bring the previously passed family members forward. When the spirit child sees them, it makes the transition into the light a lot easier on the spirit.

I told him that it was time to go and asked him if he was ready this time. This time he said yes, and he gave me a long hug. I took his tiny hands and put him with the angels. I knew that he had connected with them. They headed for the light. He was finally going home. 10:30 p.m.

The Flamingo

It started out being a regular Friday night. We were going out to meet friends that had assisted on the closing of the vortex. I had been in the shut away in the den writing my book. I needed to get out for a while.

We started that night at a local sports bar called Pockets. One of the friends that Kathleen worked with was having a Birthday Party. This place is like any other sports bar, with large pool tables, not the ones you pay as you go. The larger table gives you more of a challenge. Immediately after entering, I could feel someone behind me.

For the bar being big on paranormal activities, the energy was good. We shot a couple of games of pool and the spirit stayed pretty close to us. Kathleen had to go pick up her cousin, but she was going to meet up with us later.

We headed to this small bar. It had an older type crowd but the entertainment was great. Not too loud, small dance floor, and gambling machine's in the back. There were couples dancing, it seemed everyone was having a great time. We took some pictures with my digital camera. As a Spirit Rescuer, the camera are my eyes to unseen dimensions. When leaving the bar, we noticed something in the picture right away. Things were quiet on the way home. The Lion and I talked about how good it was to see Kathleen and Jordan.

The next morning I woke up, got on the computer and started checking out the pictures we had taken the night before. I was interested to see if anything had attached to Jordan. We had noticed something in the photo the night before. Our Marlys has a powerful gift of reading photographs. We noticed orbs in some of the pictures, although skeptics would say it could be dust on the lens. The picture of Jordan has a streak in the image. According to Marlys, it was a spirit.

Marlys message:

I knew that the spirit had followed us to The Flamingo. What we didn't know was, who they were and what they wanted.

 My impression was that the young boy had been cruising with his friend's, joyriding, typical teenagers, drinking having a good time. Donny, a 16 year old boy, was the driver. He had also had been drinking. 2 other boys were his passengers. Sherman and another 16 year old, Frankie. The car had flipped with the teenagers inside, catching on fire. Donny and Sherman had passed into the light. Frankie on the other hand had not. During the accident, he had received a blow to his head, but that wasn't what killed him. The smoke and fire did. He was alone and scared in the dark. The bright light he had responded to was me. Frankie wanted to be reunited with his family and friends. I emailed Marlys back and asked her to tell Frankie I was waiting to help him and asked if she could direct him here. All he had to do was follow my voice. I kept focusing on him, inviting him to me. Only a brief wait, then we noticed a change in the air.

He stood in the living room by the door. He was a shy boy, only 16 years old. He just wanted to be at peace. Donny had come through to welcome him. Waiting along with Donny were Frankie's Grandparents. He was eager to go. I called on the angels and sent him up immediately. There were no struggles, no pushing him, he went in easily in peace.

Little Bear

Today we had plans to run some much needed errands. The Lion and I were getting ready to take a trip to Huntington Beach, California, in a month. My daughter had moved out there 9 months earlier. She and her husband was stationed at Dyess Air Force Base in Abilene, Texas, but her husband had recently ended his time in the service. My son-in-law had been away from his home 3 years now and moved back to California. My Grandson was a couple of months old when they had moved. We are heading there, for his first Birthday, and to do some much needed R & R. We found out my daughter lived 5 minutes from the beach, I told the Lion I didn't care; I could spend my whole time at the beach. It would be a slice of heaven, a good way to ground. Get in touch with my inner self.

I got up pretty early, headed for the shower, ready when the Lion returned back to the hub of the den. The first thing on the list was to get me a new ID. Anchorage Airport had somehow lost my ID when I was checking in my luggage. It had bounced off the attendant's badge, and never was never found. With Airport security, I knew I had to replace it. I was online checking my email. While I waited for the Lion, I checked my email. Marlys had sent me one, with the subject line: Little Bear, I immediately opened it.

She stated she was drinking coffee and watching an airliner when she got the name of Little Bear. He had followed the Lion and I home from mom's she said. He was a timid child only six years old. His spirit resided near the creek behind the house. We had been doing ongoing rescues there. He was telling Marlys he wanted to find his mommy and that her name was Morning Flower, she was in the light. He had been searching for her, but he had been led to me. Little Bear is a gentle spirit, not easily to detect. He went to Marlys, knowing I could help him. He was in the hub of the den by the front door, waiting patiently, not wanting to disturb or scare me. We knew Morning Flower was in the light, so I called out to her. I called on the angels, put on the song "In the arms of the Angels." I called to Little Bear and told him that it was ok, I knew he was here. He eagerly jumped on my lap. He was the sparkle in his mother's eyes. He hunted bugs, just a typical boy. He'd show his mother, a nasty old bug which curled her toes. When he was younger, he ate them. He'd chase chickens and played with a couple of dogs that were in the camp. A very happy, normal little boy. When the song was over I knew that his mom was here. I put him in the arms of the angels, and he is now reunited with his family. I emailed Marlys back and told her what had happened.

The Lion got home around 1 that afternoon, we headed out. Today was my boss, Lydia's funeral. We were going to be in Ft. Worth, so we decided to shoot some pictures of the creek. If there was one needing the light, then more will follow.

We arrived back to the apartment late afternoon. Back on to the computer, I found that Marlys had sent another email. We already knew that there were 28 rescues left at the creek, some spirits lurk there, so we are taking the Indian children and that they would come to me. They had seen what happened with the Little Bear and his family and were lining up for my help. She said the rescues were going to pick up and many are waiting and many, many more needed our help- they just didn't know it. Some are being held captured by nasties. She was getting messages from all over the creek. She said the Lion and I would need to be rested, because in her own words " there will be a boat load "of rescue's when we got back! It will feel almost like a 24/7 job! Extremely busy! This was the perfect timing. Simply amazes me about the timing. The angels, how things are in Divine Order as they should be. Rested, we can precede forward, and on to the next rescue.

Chapter Six
Family in Need
Ross Cemetery

I had a very unusual Spirit Rescue with the spirit of an elderly gentlemen. It was a different from my usual experience. A Grandfather, named Mr. Herwood, came through to me. I saw him as a gentle soul, who drank Canadian Mist and loved to eat chicken. He hangs out with The Lion at his apartment. The Lion acknowledged his presence, which I feel made it easier for Albert to come through.

The first night I was in the apartment, I met Mr. Herwood (Grandfather). Sitting down at the dinner table to eat, he stood in between The Lion and me. Grandfather was a gentle soul, and I felt nothing, but positive energy during my visit. I feel that Grandfather might have been there to check me out, because of my work as a light worker.

One weekend, we decided to take a trip out to Abilene. We wanted to go see The Lion's daughter, Cassandra, who is 8 months pregnant with his first grandchild. The Lion's Aunt lives in Clyde, Texas a small farming community in Callahan County. It is about a 2 hour drive from Fort Worth. It was so comical, that shortly after explaining to The Lion's Mom, Berta, and his daughter about watching for signs of paranormal activity, such as movement out of the corner of their eye, smells and things missing or moved, The Lion's Aunt Bea walked in. Aunt Bea asked, "What about catching glimpses of Herwood?" She had seen him out of the corner of her eye, and occasionally felt him sitting on the bed next to her from time to time.

After explaining the way paranormal works, and describing exactly what I do as a Spirit Rescuer, Aunt Bea asked me about the encounters with Herwood. I confirmed that she was right. Herwood was going back and forth between dimensions and family members homes. He enjoys being in a place where he is acknowledged.

The next day, Sunday, we took the 10 minute trip to Baird. It was a clear Sunday afternoon, around 3 p.m. it was windy, but the temperature a nice 78 degrees, a beautiful day In Texas. Before going to the cemetery, I was given a short tour of Main Street. Baird is a quaint little city. It is the second County Seat for Callahan County. The County Seat was moved to Baird when the railroad bypassed the original County Seat, Belle Plains. I was shown where Herwood's store once stood, and where his first office was. The Lion's Mom also took us by the Texas and Pacific Train Depot. It seems that Grandfather retired from the railroad, before he became a business owner. I was also taken to the family home where all the children had grown up, and generations had come there for all the family gatherings. After seeing where the family lived, we then pulled into the Cemetery in Baird where the family was buried.

The Lion's Grandmother, and Frank Carroll, her son, are buried side by side. Frank had taken his own life a few years ago. As we pulled into Ross Cemetery, I noticed how big it was. I think it had to be the only cemetery in this small town. The cemetery sits on both sides of US

Highway 283. The cemetery dates back to the 1800's, when the City of Baird was chartered. It also has a historical marker.

After pulling into the cemetery, I was first led to clear the outside of the perimeter. Nasty spirits were lingering there. They were unable to enter this sacred place, but could convince the trapped spirits to come out of the peacefulness of the cemetery to join them. Starting with my Arch Angel Michael Invocation, I proceeded to clear the perimeter. Due to the huge size of the cemetery, I directed all my attention to the west side of the cemetery today, as that is where the Family members are interned. I do plan to go back and go through the entire cemetery at a later date, but today was about Family.

The spirit guides directed me around the cemetery. I was being led to several of the children's markers. My guides told me that there were some children that needed to go into the light, but that was not my foremost mission today. I acknowledged each of them, and agreed they all would go into the light safely as well.

After about 20 minutes of exploration, I was led to the Grandmother's Grave. Her name was Georgie Elizabeth Turner she went by (Lizzie). She is buried next to Frank. I picked up on Frank's spirit right away - he was very angry. He had been told in life that he had a tumor. On top of his illness, he had some major family problems going on at home. Frank died of a self-inflicted gunshot wound. He would have been turning 50. Due to his anger, he had never gone into the light. I explained to the family that the Grandmother had gone into the light, but she had come back to the cemetery to watch over the spirit of Frank.

While visiting with Frank, he had several messages for me to share. First, he told me that he was sorry. He wanted me to let the family members know how sorry he really was. He also wanted me to let his sisters know he was there. He wanted to hug each of them before going into the light. He hugged me and said thank you.

As he hugged me, I could feel myself being lifted up into the air. In life, he must have been a very tall man! I then went to the family and gave them Frank's messages. I told them that they needed to get ready to tell him goodbye. One by one, they did. I helped them to feel his presence, by putting their hands underneath mine, and letting them feel his energy. He indeed, was there. With the Arch Angels on standby, we sent Frank into the light. Upon helping Frank go into the light, the Grandmother was now at peace, and able to go where she needed to see her loved ones.

As for Herwood, the Grandfather, he actually went back to the house with us. We all could feel his presence there. Grandpa still hangs around at The Lion's apartment occasionally and his presence has also been felt at The Lion's cousin's house in Haltom City, Texas as well. Recently he has been in Clyde most of the time with the Sisters since they both are now acknowledging him. Frank in time will be back, I believe this. The way he took his life will be forgiven. The stage was set by others and the uncontrollable circumstances around him; all he did was end the misery that he was in. Granted this is not the answer, but in the state of mind he was in, he saw no other way to ease the pain and anger.

The spiritual children, I had communicated with, came home with me. They hung out with us at the house for a couple hours. Children like to spend time around me, before I send them to the light. They need to put their trust in me. When crossing over to the light, trust in the facilitator and assists their transition and makes it occur much easier. I have found that patience is the best way to help a child to cross, especially if they have been in the dark for a long time. I sent them peacefully on their way as the sun was going down.

As a Spirit Rescuer, I can relate so much with the lost souls searching for the light. Like them, I have learned, it is better to be one with the light, than lose my way in the dark.

The Lion's Grandmothers Headstone Baird Cemetery

The Lion, Aunt Bea and the Lion's mom Berta

Final resting place of Lizzie, she helped with the rescue
of her Son

Showing Aunt Bea the energy coming off of the headstone

Chapter Seven
Rescue of an American Soldier
Admiral Cemetery

Fort Worth

On a very cold, Thanksgiving morning, we left Fort Worth around ten a.m. We were going west on Interstate 20 to Thurber. Around 10:50 a.m. we entered Gordon, Texas, the town before Thurber. I noticed, that I tended to get visitors (spirit children) every time I go that direction! Abilene was a frequent destination for me. I have to go through Thurber to get to Abilene. I noticed there was some heaviness in the car; we had picked up a couple of spirits my coffee cup seemed heavy, as well as the clipboard on which I was writing. I knew a Spirit Rescue was about to happen. We were listening to a CD. I thought the occasion called for the appropriate music, so I forwarded the CD to Brookes and Dunn's, "I Believe"- a good Spirit Rescue song. The music had been in alignment with the upcoming rescue. "Only God Knows Why," by Kidd Rock was on before.

It amazes me, that no matter where I go, or what I do, I pick up the spirit vibrations immediately.

Even though we were just passing near the cemetery, the energy was very intense! As we got closer, I opened the portal to send them to the light. The energy vibration greatly increased. One of the lost children went straight to the light. Two required my assistance. I had to give a slight push to help them through. The last, was a little boy around two years old. He didn't want to go to the light. I did not push him to go to the light. Instead, we let him go with us. I knew that after he had spent some time with us, trust will develop and we could send him to the light later, when we returned home through Thurber.

The Lion's Grandfather had hitched a ride with us, and was sitting in the back seat. He loved Thanksgiving, the time for family and turkey. We were curious to see how the Lion's Mom would react. This was going to be a good day for healing the family. Grandpa was saying, "She is not making any effort to forgive me". The Lion's Mom, Berta, has not made her mind on whether or not to forgive the Grandfather. I don't expect her forgiveness anytime soon, although she is trying and making great strides. Frankie, will not be with the family today. We sent him to the light only a couple of weeks ago, so he would still be in healing at this time.

After we ate a great Thanksgiving dinner, the Lion, his three daughters and I jumped in the car. We traveled up the road, four miles to Admiral Cemetery. When we first pulled up to the cemetery, we got a sense of peacefulness, even on the perimeter outside the fence. Just to be cautious, I went ahead and cleared the negative energy, using the Archangel Michael prayer. After the blessing, the Lion, Cassandra and I proceeded inside. Sara and Ava decided to wait in the car. They felt it was too cold to be out in the wind. It had started snowing.

This was another cemetery with a Historical marker. It dated back to the 1880's. There are a lot soldiers buried here. Outside the gate, there is a plaque listing all the names of the soldiers buried here. The soldiers are listed by the war in which they had served. The list of causes included the Confederate Army, Spanish American War, WWI, WWII, Korea and Vietnam.

Upon entering, I was immediately greeted by a spirit and led to the far front side of the cemetery. My first impression was that I was being led to the perimeter, but I was mistaken. I was guided to a grave. The foot marker had a T.S. on it. Her name was Thelma Smith, and she died at the age of 9 months in 1913.

Meanwhile, Cassandra, the Lion's daughter, was being led to another part of the cemetery. She has recently discovered her gifts as a Spirit Rescuer. I was then led to the back of the cemetery, to a couple more children's markers, and then to the far side. Cassandra and I crossed paths and headed in opposite directions. Immediately after the direction change, I came across a pair of markers resting side by side. They were two sets of twins, one stone listed DJ and RL. I was not able to decipher the names on the other headstones from the photos. As I am also a twin, I felt certain this was a sign! I was lead in circles around the tree and the headstones.

I got restless and walked the same path, at least four times, waiting on Cassandra to finish up, so we could get pictures.

As I was planning to leave, I walked towards the front of the cemetery. I was almost to the gate when I was stopped again. The headstone that had caught my eye, was of a soldier, a Private who served in the Army Air Corps during WWII- "Pvt. George E. Lincecum June 7, 1913 – February 17, 1974." He was here at the cemetery. He had never crossed over! I immediately asked him if he was ready to go. He said yes. I went ahead and called on the Angels to take him. He gave me a hug goodbye, lifting me almost off the ground! I have noticed that several of the spirits tend to do that with me. At the moment I sent him to the light, Ava got out of the car. She told me she saw a "weird gust of wind" go straight upward at the moment that was I sending him to the Light. Cassandra was still being led by spirits, so I went ahead. and went to the car for a while.

They were finally done shooting pictures. As she was leaving, she jokingly said, "whoever needs to go to the light, come on!" In retrospect, she realizes it was a big mistake with a potential for anything! Luckily for all of us, the cemetery was peaceful and very positive, so we did not have to deal with any malicious spirits, just three children that answered Cassandra's offer of assistance.

As we went back through Thurber, I sent the three children summoned by Cassandra into the Light. Sometime before we got to Thurber, the Lion had put the CD with "I Believe" on it, back into the player. While I was trying to convince the hesitant two year old that it was safe to go with the Angels, that song was again playing. I told the young boy the story that I read to scared children who need my help. It seemed to help, he finally let go and went with the Angels into the Light.

A month later, on Christmas Eve, the Lion and I, returned to the Admiral Cemetery to pay our respects. As we entered the cemetery, the air was again very peaceful. I was immediately led around in a circle, searching. Sometimes that happens, before we get clearer communication set up and on the right track. I was taken back to the front gate, so I again called on Archangel Michael for protection and to clear the area. We left the entrance, and traveled to the middle of the cemetery. We walked down the middle of the cemetery straight back to the fence. Again, we went to the Grave of DJ and RL and the two markers by the tree. Then we went to the row of children. They were buried in a perfect row, the graves slightly mounded up. There were quite a few children in that area, all different ages. Some as young as a day old, babies, many by the same family, some were toddlers, just two or three years old that had died of different illnesses. We wanted to pay our respects, so we placed a single flower, and wished them a Merry Christmas. It just seemed right to us. After all, it was the night before Santa Claus comes.

As a tribute to the soldiers that had served and fought so bravely. We placed red flowers on all of the service men's graves. The Lion and I, had both served in the military. We wanted them to know that even though gone, they were not forgotten. It was a very emotional moment. You could feel the thankfulness and warmth as we were doing this. Some of these graves you could tell hadn't had a visit in quite a while. They needed a little maintenance and TLC. During this visit, I repaired a wreath that had come loose from one of the older markers in the cemetery. This experience left the Lion and I feeling very much in the Christmas Spirit, the first time this season. Knowing that all of these forgotten people had been acknowledged was a very rewarding and uplifting way to spend the holidays

Rescue of an American Soldier Admiral Cemetery

The graves of children lined up in formation!

The Headstone of the Soldier Rescued

Chapter Eight
Rescue of Sally Ann
Smithfield Cemetery

The Haunting of Sierra Sky

Our first trip out to the Smithfield Cemetery, was on a cold New Year's day, January 1, 2008. I encountered a mixed bag of feelings as I walked around. Some parts of the cemetery were peaceful, yet, there were other parts that were very heavy. The conflicting messages I was receiving is hard to describe. We noticed that a lot of the grave markers had a story behind them. We could see various spiritual imprints on the headstones. One, showed a woman with a baby in the fetal position. Another one revealed, an image of lips, and a face which had the face disfigured. In another picture there was a woman weeping by the tree alone, looking for her boys.

The darker part of the cemetery revealed many souls that had not gone to their final resting place. Souls not at rest are troubled, bringing disturbance and unbalance to a place. Marlys shared with us that there was a woman with strong feelings of abandonment, who cries out. There were men hanging by a clump of trees watching us with curiosity, with their guns hanging from their belt. Some of the negative energy we were picking up, is the energy of static souls that have unrest around them at the time of their death. The conditions at the Smithville Cemetery showed signs of neglect; you could see some of the resting places hardly have visitors. The deeper we got into the cemetery you could see that there had been a lot of vandalism on the grounds. It was very sad to see the many headstones that had been broken, just lying around, neglected and forgotten. Was there even a caretaker here?

We decided that we wanted to try to retrieve additional information from some of the headstones that were hard to read. We started with a headstone marked "Henderson." We chose green and proceeded to try and get some additional information. We read, "James A. and T.A Henderson", 9 year old little girl born in the late 1800's. I decided to take a picture of the grave to see if I could capture any information using a camera. Out of respect for the dead, I always ask for permission first, before I shoot a picture. I sent Marlys a copy of the photo and while viewing it, she felt a lot of heaviness, but no specific information. Next we moved on to a marker with "Hargrove" on it. We got a bad feeling from the residual energies that surrounded this marker. The marker showed that the Hargrove's had lost their babies.

A large area of the cemetery is filled with dark forces. The force is so strong, it also encompasses a large area outside the cemetery fence. There are four men buried in the dark section, who murdered Native American men, woman and children. They set fire to a covered wagon, destroying the family sleeping inside for their money and jewelry. These twisted men enjoyed torturing innocent people and causing their deaths. Their evil souls never regretted the horrors, that they had spread in the territory. A legion of dark spirits was attracted to the hateful, villainous ways of the murderers and has joined with them. Eventually, some brave men caught up with these murderers and executed them. Even though their lives were extinguished, their spirits remained earthbound, still hurting living people and animals that got too close to their burial sites. They still are taking joy in whatever pain they can inflict upon the living.

One morning, we were heading to Richardson, Texas a suburb of Dallas. We had plans to attend a meeting on an upcoming investigation event at a place known as the Spiritual Center. Before leaving for Richardson, I received an email from Marlys. For two days she had been hearing a child crying. On the second day, She asked the child, "What is your name?" The child said, "Sally Ann." She asked her age. Marley then called Sierra and told her that we have another rescue. I gave Sierra all the information I was able to get out of Sally Ann. She is a strawberry blonde, little girl that has green eyes that sparkled when she smiled. I sent Sally Ann's spirit to Sierra and told her to stay with her and do what Sierra says.

Sally Ann was a 3 year old that had climbed up the ladder in the barn and fell from the loft. She had broken her neck in the fall. She was crying out to Marlys for help, but we weren't sure of which cemetery she was buried in. We knew we wanted to help, but we had to find her gravesite first. Marlys followed the cries and located her at the Smithfield Cemetery. Before we could do anything to help her, we had to make sure that she was with us. Before leaving to go to Richardson, I emailed Marlys back, and explained; only after we left our den would we be able to call the little girl to us through a song. As we were leaving the hub of the den, on the way to the car, we spotted a trail of little white feathers; we have been seeing them a lot outside the Hub.

Pulling out of the parking area, I decided to put on some music to call out to Sally Ann. I have compiled a CD of songs that I use for different rescues. The song I chose today was Lonely Road of Faith by Kid Rock. I started the song and started to call Sally Ann. Almost immediately we knew she was there with us. The Lion at times could feel her touching his hand. We felt a good energy in the car that had not been there before.

We had a spirit that was no longer in the dark, she was with us and safe.

She sat in between us on the way as we talked. She loved to hear me sing the different songs I was playing. One of the questions I asked was if she saw the angels, she replied yes. I asked if she was ready to go to the light, or if she wanted to be with us for a while. She chose to go with us to the Spiritual Center. When we got to Richardson, we realized that we had another passenger with us, Little Feather was in the car. Before we headed into the building, I told the kids that under no circumstances were they to leave the room. This was a Spiritual Center and the atmosphere was peaceful and positive.

After completing out meeting, we headed back to the Smithfield Cemetery to look for Sally Ann's marker. When we arrived at the Cemetery it was getting late almost 6 p.m. our time. There was a chill in the air at sundown, so we didn't have a lot to time. When we pulled in, we both were immediately led back to the place we were at the last visit. We walked around looking for her marker, but were having a hard time finding it. This is an old Cemetery and some of the headstones didn't have markers that could be easily read. We also noticed that the headstones that told us a story before, were not as detailed this time. Little Feather and Sally Ann had a good time taking me around in circles. Marlys had told me that the marker with the double humps looked like the headstone of Sally Ann. We called her in the arms of the angels about 6p.m and Little Feather was by her side. She is no longer trapped in the dark and can enjoy the peaceful serenity of the eternal light. She is up there playing with the other children, and Little Feather made a friend that day.

We took pictures at the cemetery that day. The atmosphere had been pleasant, but there were still areas that give you a bad feeling as well. While we were out there, some of the photographs taken that day, suggest that we were not alone. My jacket looks like it had been ripped with a claw mark. We hadn't gone under any fences, but you can see in one of the pictures that there is one claw mark on the back of my jacket. We still haven't returned to Smithfield Cemetery and gone over in that direction as of yet, but have plans to do so.

The Smithfield Cemetery

The Henderson Headstone

The back of my jacket I went home with a claw mark!

The Hargrove babies Marlys got a bad pain in the chest

Chatting with a spirit before sending him to the light

Chapter Nine
Cartersville, Texas

I wanted to end my book with the investigation we are currently working on. I first worked with Justin in Pennsylvania. Through my visitation with his Great-Great-Grandfather and through pictures. I had visited the cemetery numerous times searching for the final resting place of his Grandfather, John Burns, an American Hero.

Justin and I have stayed in touch briefly through emails and through a yahoo group we are both members of. In April of this year, I received an email from him, requesting help from my team. They had some paranormal activity going on. He told me that he would not go into details about the location, nor tell me anything about what has been happening there. He told me that he did not want my mind to have any preconceived ideas, I agreed. The Lion and I would go in without knowing anything about the location. They had been using his wife, Kristina, to channel through. He told me that Kristina, had been getting strong EVP's of at least four different people.

After discussing it with Marlys and the Lion, we decided to go in and help. We set up the investigation for the following Monday. Cartersville was located eight miles on the other side of Springtown. We were to meet Justin at a local grocery store and then follow him to the location. We arrived early, so we decided to eat dinner at a local restaurant. We finished just in time to meet Justin. He explained where we were going. The Lion knew exactly where this place was located. The Lion used to live not too far from Cartersville, now called Carter.

Carter was founded just after the Civil War 1866-67. The city got its name from Judge Carter, one of the three men who founded the community. In 1888, the town opened a Post Office that stayed open until 1907. The Post Office still stands, although it has been converted into a home. The Red Dog Saloon is still there. This too, is now a home. The two structures still standing are an open air Tabernacle and the old town Church. Carter was the location of the last Indian raid in Parker County, that occurred in 1874. There is a lot of history in this former mill town which is now a ghost town.

By the time we got there Justin's wife, Kristina, and her mother Cynthia, were setting up their equipment. We talked for a few minutes outside of the location before entering. The afternoon was beautiful with perfect weather; we arrived there just as the sun was going down. The first building we went into was the church. The church was abandoned of living people, however, it is a hot spot for the paranormal. Many other investigative teams had been out here. The church was donated to the community and proudly standing on the land with several historical markers describing the events that had happened in the past. Entering the church I got a peaceful feeling. I went in and quietly sat in the back pew. I was not saying anything. I wanted to get a feeling for my surroundings and just waited to see what might come to me.

Kristina was watching the video camera and on the monitor, she noticed many orbs starting to gather around the Lion and myself. On the way to Cartersville, I had gotten the name Sara. I told the Lion that she was a little girl that was out there.

In previous investigations of Cartersville, Cynthia's great grandson had brought forth the spirits and captured messages from them on a tape recorder. He is 13 years old and has the gift of sensitivity passed down on Cynthia's side of the family. They had captured several EVPs.

Finally, everyone came into the church and seated themselves in different pews. We discussed the EVPs from the earlier visit. They had captured on the recordings a woman named Esther, but I did not feel her presence at the time. They had also recorded the voice of a little girl. I shared with them the name of this little girl, Sara. I wanted our focus to be on Sara and reuniting her with her father, who had already gone to the light.

As we sat there talking, I called to Sara. She came forward immediately and took my hands. Sara has not been allowed to leave the church. The last thing her father had told her to do was to stay inside, therefore she felt trapped inside the church. I shared Sara's presence with Kristina by using my hands to guide hers to Sara. You could feel pure joy coming from this delightful spirit. We talked to Sara for a while. We found out that she was four years old, she had freckles, hazel eyes and she wore her long auburn-almost red, hair, in pigtails not braided. She wears a full apron over her dress. She wears black, high top shoes and long, white stockings. She is missing one of her baby teeth in the front.

I wanted to go outside and see if the orb activity within the church declined when I was not there. I promised Sara that I would not abandon her, I would be back, I just needed to step outside for a few moments. I told her that she needed to stay in the church.

After leaving the church, I headed to Justin's vehicle to view the activity on the small monitor screen Justin and Kristina had hooked up in the back seat of their car.

Justin asked me to go check out the perimeter of the fence line. In a previous investigation, a skeptic of paranormal activity felt like they had been pushed. I noticed a small tree out on the far right of the perimeter. I got the feeling that someone died out there. Justin later told me that a man had come onto the land and shot the owner. A battle erupted and the intruder was wounded, then rode off. There is a historical marker describing the incident including the direction in which the man rode off in. Justin had read the marker, but I had not, so Justin was getting the validation he needed.

I felt, I was now surrounded by many spirits. I could hear the laughter of children all over the property. Running, playing, enjoying what life had to offer them. It was starting to get late, and we had an hour drive home after we loaded up the equipment. We went back inside of the church. You could feel the harmony and the peace that this place represented. Our conclusion is that the spirits were happy here. Many of them have already gone into healing, but would come back to visit since it represented a happier time. It was time to send Sara home into the light. I called on Archangel Michael to escort her to the family that were waiting in the light for her.

As we said goodbye, I told Justin and the others, that I would be in touch. As the Lion and I drove home, we compared notes. This place has a history of love, compassion, harmony and peace. There had been bloodshed at the location and the land showed it. However, the church acted as a sanctuary and had kept the peaceful energies inside of its walls.

After we got home, I sent the pictures of Cartersville to Marlys for her impressions. She also received information on the little girl, Sara. Marlys shared with me that Sara had loved to play with dolls, although she only had one to play with, a very old doll. She had a brother named Daniel, who was four years older. Daniel had been a typical, rough housing, little boy. He had red, curly hair with a ready smile on his face. He was seen wearing brown trousers, black shoes and a white shirt. Daniel loved to climb trees and go fishing. He was a help to his father, John, with planting crops, taking care of the animals, and helping his father with repairs to the wagon. He also helped his mother around the house.

Daniel and Sara's Mother was named Katie May. Like most families of that era, Sara helped her mother with baking, collecting eggs, and setting the table. Katie May helped her children with their Sunday school lessons and homework.

John, the head of the house, was husband to Katie May, and father to Sara and Daniel. He did not make his money as a business man, but as a farmer. He provided for his family with the crops he grew in his fields. He worked hard keeping food on the table and a roof over his beloved families head. Times were hard, but they survived. He was a hard worker and appreciated everything his family did to help him. The little family enjoyed church on Sundays. They attended the picnics that often followed the Sunday services and attended many of the church socials. This family left us with several impressions; self-sufficiency, pride in a job well done, loyalty to each other, and living the American dream.

The following Sunday, we decided to do a follow up investigation. The investigative team would be made up of two of Justin's members and two of mine. In preparation for the next investigation, we had listened to the EVP's that we had recorded on the previous visit. Much to our surprise, we had the little girl, Sara, on the tape, before sending her to the light. Hearing Sara, reconfirmed with us that the spirits at the church needed to communicate with us. We were ready to assist anyway that we could.

We planned to meet Justin at one o'clock in the afternoon. The sky was dark and rain had been forecast. The Lion and I were the first to reach the church. We went ahead and went into the church. We wanted to start the tape recorder while it was still quiet. I knew that Sara had gone on to the light, so we weren't expecting to hear her. However, we had heard lots of laughter, on the last visit. We knew there would be more children, and we were hoping to capture the sounds of their laughter on tape.

Justin and Kristina arrived at one thirty. We greeted them, and gave them time to set up their equipment. Today, they were using the infrared camera and recording video. Justin and Kristina had previously conducted many recording sessions inside this church using both sound and video equipment. While they set up, Kristina told me that an investigation team from Dallas had been out here the night before. This place is indeed a paranormal hotspot for the curious!

This time, the church, was not as active as it had been the preceding Monday night, however, a spirit came forth as I walked in the door. I told Justin that there was a little boy standing in the corner, as you first walk through the doors. He was alone, a small child, very young, probably about five years old. I was hearing the name William, but was not connecting the name with the little boy.

We took some pictures inside the church to forward to Marlys so that she could read them. Marlys told us that the big orb in the picture was Esther. She was a cranky, old woman- the type that would throw things across the room when provoked. We had noticed her in the previous investigation as well. Marlys also had information on who the little boy in the corner was. His name is Tommy Lufkin's- five years old; Marlys went on to explain that he was a handful. He loves running, climbing trees and getting into mischief. He would play tricks on the little girls, which resulted in his spending a lot of time in the corner, during school! I then understood why I had felt him in a corner! Tommy was just your typical, mischievous little boy. Tommy would stay in the church/school and clean up afterwards. The teacher felt Tommy should be disciplined when he did things wrong. Although she was strict with him, Tommy liked his teacher, and made a point to finding out that her name was Izzy. He sometimes would pick wild flowers to give to her. He just could not resist a fight, rolling around in the dirt wrestling with another boy. Tommy could be wailing on someone, and in the next moment, gently holding a pup in his arms, talking softly to it.

Justin asked me if I was feeling anything else especially concerning the history of the church. He had some names, he wanted further information about. I told him the number 1874 was coming up. We knew that the church was here during that time. I went outside, the spirit of a man immediately greeted me. He led me to a marker by the church. The marker described a shooting incident that had taken place in 1874. This spirit also took me to the edge of the road where there was another memorial marker, displaying the names of seven men called "The Seven Rugged Riders" that had lived in the area. One of the names was Will Curry (William). Another one of the names listed was Bryant Prather. Mr. Prather was a minister and a historian.

Prather Road is named for him. It is located not far from the church.

William was a stern man, yet could be nice. There are a few men he does not like, and he calls them troublemakers. A good husband, but with a hair-trigger temper when he is around certain men. He helped make repairs on the church when a storm caused damage. He could found in the local saloon. He witnessed a few shootings over cheating in a game.

Along the perimeter of the fence there were men leaning up against trees, shotguns in their hands, watching us on every investigation. Indians were out in the field mounted on their horses, making their way closer to the church. We were learning that during that era, throughout Texas, Cowboys and Indians had been fighting in an ongoing battle. There was also something else that watched in the field, as of now, we have no clue what is out there, but, we all came to the conclusion that it was not demonic. That afternoon we did not stay long. With the other investigation team there the day before, we wanted to let things settle.

The Lion's daughter, Cassandra was driving from Abilene into Fort Worth, to meet a friend, that was in the service. Cassandra reminds me a lot of myself when I was starting out. She has the gifts of clairvoyance and is learning from me how to Spirit Rescue. I decided, that after five years of learning, it was time for me to help people that are starting on their path. The purpose of this book was to put the word out there, that people are not alone. If you need assistance, paranormally speaking, there are many places to turn to for help. Cassandra had been keeping up with the investigations of Cartersville. She was eager to go with us. She was especially intrigued, since the Lion and his two daughters lived not too far from the location.

It was a clear, Sunday afternoon, in the beginning of May 2008. She met with us, and together we rode to Cartersville. Cassandra was excited! She has been on a couple of investigations with us, starting with Admiral

Cemetery, and has been fascinated with the paranormal ever since. She dove right in to Spirit Rescue just as she always does when she finds a topic that captures her interest. She went into the church to watch The Lion set up the laptop to start audio recording. She then started exploring the Tabernacle. She opened a room that houses a piano. She took several pictures and as she was trying to close the door, it was stuck. She reopened the door, and told whoever was in there to come out if they wanted to. She was then able to close the door without any trouble. After looking at the pictures she took in the room, you could see an orb.

Cassandra and I left the church and walked the perimeter of the fence. I explained to her what we had perceived standing in this spot on the earlier visit. She told me that she could also feel turmoil, fighting, arguing and gunfire. The land had a lot of anger and bloodshed.

Cassandra had brought her son Taylor, with her to the church that day. He has a very peaceful look about him.

Occasionally you could catch him looking over our heads. He would also just gaze into thin air. As if watching a friend, or seeing someone familiar. To entertain the little one, the Lion took him for a walk in the stroller. Taylor always enjoys his walks, but today you could hear him cooing. I think he was talking to the spirits there at Carter. I can now say I was there when Taylor went on his first investigation! I am laughing as I write this, as I remember Cassandra being pregnant with him at the investigation at Admiral Cemetery. I am sure this is the beginning of a long list of investigations for our Lion Cub, Taylor. Cassandra is so in tune with the paranormal, and The Cub is a being of the light also. When we left, he got a little fussy. I think he felt comfortable at the little country church in Carter.

After knowing about Tommy Lufkin, we knew we would have to return to Cartersville one more time. We needed to perform a Spirit Rescue for Tommy, the little boy that I have seen previously standing in the corner of the room.

We had a busy week ahead of us. Our 16 month old Grandson was visiting from California while his mom and dad were in Abilene, spending time with their friends. Keeping the toddler, allowed the Lion and myself to spend some quality time with our Grandson. We decided to take him back to his parents over Memorial weekend, which would give us a chance to get together with our daughters as well. Since we would be near Carter, I called Justin to let him know that we would be in his area if they wanted to meet us. I would rather do the investigation with his team. He has started the ball rolling on the work in Carter, and I just felt like this was Justin's baby. He deserved that respect as a fellow ghost hunter and friend. I felt they needed to be with us every step of the way. We originally set the investigation for Monday, Memorial Day; we would be traveling home from Abilene and could take the short cut through the town of Weatherford.

The day before we were supposed to return home, the Lion and I spent too much time at the pool. The heat index on this day was peaking well into the 100's and we had gotten a severe sun burn! By the time, we made it back to the room, all we could think about was going home. We said our goodbye's to our daughters and headed back to North Richland Hills. When we woke up Monday morning, the sunburn had done it's damage. The Lion and I were both very uncomfortable, cringing with the thought of wearing clothes. We were miserable, but knew that we had to go on with the investigation. We had to get to the church and save this little boy. I called Justin explaining what had happened. We asked if we could meet them in the early evening after the sun had gone down.

I told the Lion that I wanted to play a song on the car radio; I felt that with the spiritual music blasting in the background, lost spirits would flee to the church. I sat down in the last pew quietly, and I waited. My focus was directed to the corner where we have previously seen Tommy. I explained to Tommy that we were sending him home, the angels were standing by, to take him into the light, reuniting this little boy with his parents who were waiting for him on the other side. We all knew from a previous investigation that there were many other children here!

Through Marlys eyes, we knew of another boy, Billy Cromwell. He was eight years old. Billy attended both school and church. When Marlys talked with the little boy he stated that he wanted to play with a ball, today this little boy indeed got his wish granted. Justin saw the ball actually move.

The Lion and Justin were shooting pictures telling us that the orb activity had increased. Marlys was right the toys had made a difference. It was now almost 8 o'clock. The Lion and I were getting tired and in pain with the sunburns, Justin was tired after pulling ten-hour shifts on his job. I walked over to the corner where Tommy was standing; it was time to send him to the light, as we prepared him for flight. You could see through the camera lens blue orbs, realizing Tommy wasn't alone. He had some friends with him, also waiting. On the other side was Sam Jordan, he was nine years old, light brown hair and just like Tommy. Sam like to antagonize the girls with neat snake skins, anything that would freak them out. He liked cats and had several on his farm. Mugsy was his first kitty and slept with him, Tommy and Sam were best friends. I called on the angels and asked Tommy if he was ready. He was eager to be reunited with his friends and family!

As we loaded the car and headed back home, we felt good about what had happened. Almost to North Richland Hills, I heard someone calling my name- there was a spirit of a little girl sitting in the backseat behind the Lion! She told me her name was Tina. We were almost home before I noticed her! Tina followed the Lion and me up the stairs walking slowly in front of us! We went ahead and let her come into our home! I could feel Tina in the bedroom with us! I asked her why she followed me home. Tina explained to me that she like playing with the toys! I told her she needed to go into the light and that her family was waiting! A few minutes later she was gone- another angel had gotten her wings.

The next day, we reviewed the photos we had taken the day before. We received a ton of additional information!

When the Lion and I pulled up at the church, Justin and Kristina were already there. Justin's wife was sitting in the sanctuary and she had her recorder set up on a nearby pew. Kristina told me that she had brought her sisters out here the day before. They were sitting in the same room when they had picked up a voice of a woman; this woman was the resident ghost, Esther. Esther was furious that Justin was sitting in her seat in the pew. He is lucky that she did not kick him, she wanted to, just so he would move. He was sitting in her favorite place, where she would observe who the parents were of the unruly children misbehaving during church services. I was carrying our pink bag, it was filled with goodies that Marlys had sent us. The bag was loaded with toys for the children. Marlys had sent them to us a couple of days before the investigation. We were anxious to scatter them throughout the church, our goal to draw the children out. Esther was upset that we had broken one of her rules by bringing toys into the church.

We brought toys for the children, to help draw them out, and WOW did it bring out all the kids. When I laid the toys out in the church, it became alive with all these darling children. Some who had been shy, began to wonder what was in the different bags the team members had. There were a few adults there watching over them, their own curiosity holding them inside the church.

The toys that we scattered around the church brought many children in, more of them were coming. The orb activity increased filling the church with the sounds of giggling and laughter and an occasional ooh's. The children were very interested in what we had brought them. The church was alive with happy squealing children very surprised to see the toys. Marlys explained two little girls in front of me holding their hands out to grasp the doll. A toddler by the name of

Molly was hanging onto my pant leg. She had long brown hair and a big white bow. Ginny wrapped her arms around my other leg, and was holding on tight, giggling. It was more of a game for them. A little boy named Howard is sitting on the floor, legs crossed, his elbows resting on his knees, face in the palms of his tiny hands, listening to me talk, and to him it was like I was telling a story! By Justin there is little girl asking him for a sip of his cold, sweet tea. There are now 10 boys sitting on the floor, playing a game of marbles, Kristina has a little girl sitting next to her, swinging her legs, while playing with a baby doll. Over in the corner, another little girl is standing by Tommy and me. I was explaining her energy to the others, including what she was wearing! A light brown dress, black shoes, and brown hair wavy! The building was full of children, more were coming from outside. Standing in the doorway was a full figure man removing his cowboy hat as he entered the building taking his seat in the back pew. Marlys went on to tell us that there were woman and children families in wagons pulling up outside! I got the feeling this was a family social. Somehow the word was getting out! Finally a woman spoke up. She was standing next to the wall, thanking us for thinking of the children, and remembering the promise that was made to one little boy by bringing them the toys. People loved coming, because of all the happiness and peace that is here.

The ever-present Esther was there, upset over the invasion of more investigators, disrupting the normal routine inside the church. She hung around me, watching and following me. Every move I made was under Esther's hostile glare. I sat on one of the pews holding a little rag doll. Little girls clustered around me, interested in holding the doll. The boys were interested in the toy cow and balls. The church came to life with the beautiful sounds of children laughing. They were happy.

We found out there were two other friends of Tommy's in the church, Stephen was one of them, he was already in the light, Miguel was the other little boy; he was not in the light. Miguel is part Mexican and part white. He is a bit shy because people always shunned him because of his mixed heritage. In Miguel's time period, a family that was different, was also an outcast by some in the community. Many people of mixed heritage, were shunned by both races. Miguel was getting the education that other Mexican kids did not. It seems like it would be a positive thing that would make his life better, but this made it harder on Miguel. Tommy, however, liked him and they soon became friends. Miguel loved school and playing with Tommy. He was not so much into scaring the girls. His father adored him and was the apple in his daddy's eyes. His father would do anything for his son and he adored his wife. Miguel would go over to Tommy's to play and he liked the kitties. He was a gentler boy. He loved fishing. Esther did not like Miguel, because he had Mexican in him. She would say awful things to his mother when she would bring something for the church picnic. The other women treated the mother with kindness and invited her to join them in things and into their homes.

Miguel is not in the light, though my wonderful team will make sure he is reunited with his family, pulling all children and family members out of the darkness, reuniting them with their loved ones in the light.

Our investigation was a success. We had captured orbs in photos resulting in great pictures, and clear EVP from our lady, Esther telling us to get out! By those that travel through the doorway another realm I know further investigations will take place in the future, but for now, the spiritual beauty that is felt here will continue and this is one place I rejoice in visiting. Another time, another place, but through all the raids, all the killings, this small patch of land holds the true spirit of love and happiness. As we put this chapter to bed, my team is aware there is more work to be done! For we are Spirit Rescuers! Warriors of the light! Our calling-to help those that are lost, find their final destination! A place called home!

Our beloved resident ghost Esther

We asked for the spirits to show themselves Cartersville

The same picture taken right after the other one

Cartersville the rescue of Tommy

The Lion in the background with me speaking to the
spirit

Made in the USA
Lexington, KY
27 October 2015